Riddles on the Rocks

a tour of selected North American rock art sites

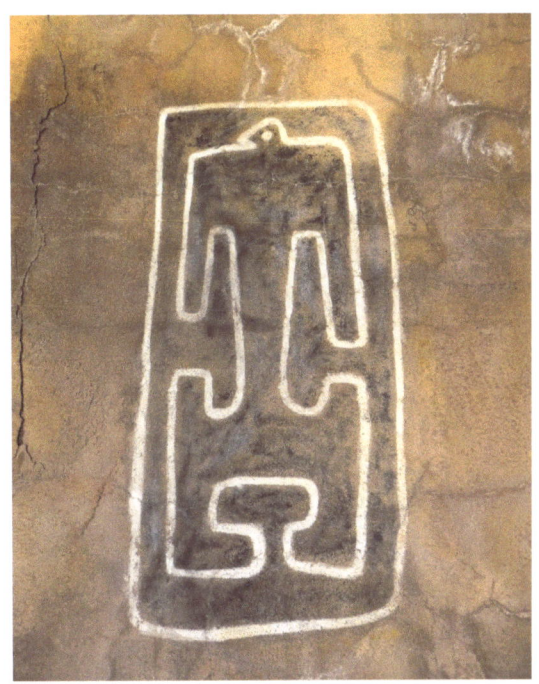

Image from Desert View Watchtower, page 37

Leon Yost

Copyright © 2014 Leon Yost
ISBN: 149953647X
ISBN-13: 9781499536478

An Exhibition of Photographs
January 6–24, 2015
Reception: Saturday, January 10, 4–6 pm

Noho-M55 Gallery
530 West 25th Street, New York, NY 10001
nohogallery.com
(212) 367-7063
Tuesdays–Saturdays, 11–6

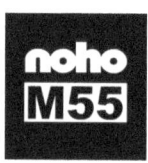

Riddles in the Rocks
Photographs in the exhibition

Dedicated to Fred Kabotie, Chester Dennis and Fred Geary

Fred Kabotie, Chester Dennis and Fred Geary worked with architect Mary Jane Colter in 1932 decorating the interior adobe walls of the Desert View Watchtower in the Grand Canyon National Park. The Fred Harvey Company employed Colter and Geary to design and furnish hotels and lodges along the Santa Fe Railway with the mission of making the long desert ride attractive for tourists from the east and west coasts. Colter designed six buildings at the Grand Canyon, one of the Santa Fe's spur destinations. She hired Hopi artists, Fred Kabotie and Chester Dennis to work along with her fellow Harvey Company employee, Fred Geary to paint the entire interior of the Watchtower with authentic Native pictographs from the Hopis and their ancestors.

Kabotie was born on Second Mesa to the Bluebird Clan in 1900 and was sent to the Santa Fe Indian School for three years when he was 15. The school's intent was to make the students "unlearn" their traditional native ways but Kabotie did just the opposite, developing an even stronger appreciation for his Hopi culture and their ceremonies. On advice from an educated Anglo friend that recognized his artistic talent and ability to recall his tribe's precise ceremonial details, he quit the Indian School and transferred to the Santa Fe Public High School for a better-balanced education.

Throughout his life he remained a traditional Hopi but also built a successful art and teaching career, copying kiva murals for the Museum of Modern Art in 1940 and earning a Guggenheim fellowship in 1945. He died in 1986. The lives of Chester Dennis and Fred Geary are less known but their work in the Desert View Watchtower demonstrates that they also were skilled artists—and the "team of three" did outstanding work together as we can see by the examples scattered throughout this booklet.

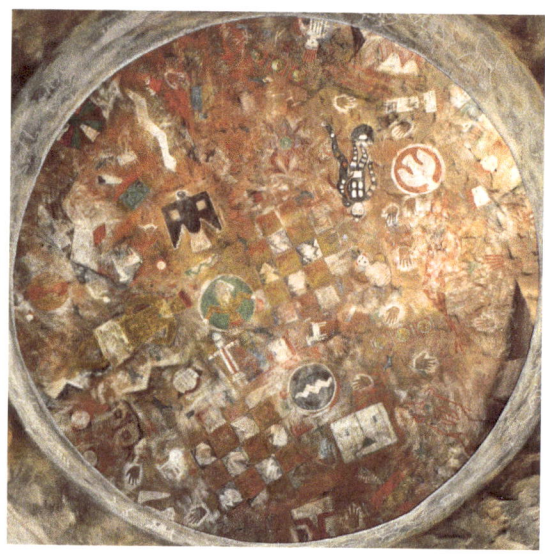

(*above*) Fred Geary painted the tower's fourth-floor ceiling with images from the Abo caves in New Mexico.

Acknowledgments

Sincere thanks to Nancy Gehman and Erma Martin Yost for their astute copyediting and design collaboration. Also, thanks to the fearless guides and archeologists who took us to impossible-to-find sites in obscure canyons: Wendy Quick, who guided us to Rochester Creek on a freezing winter morning; Johnson John, who lives in and guided us through Slim Canyon; Daniel Staley, for his dependable guide work through the canyons of the Navajo Nation; Chuck Zehnder, who knows every corner of Nine Mile Canyon better than anyone we've ever met; Ranger Russ Bodnar, who navigated the steep trails of Canyon de Chelly like the back of his hand; Joe Pachak and Bill Davis, the resident archeology experts of Bluff, Utah; James Copeland, who drew us the essential map of the Largo Canyon area, Jim Duffield, maker of the most meticulous maps we've ever seen—dozens of them have saved us over the decades; Polly and Curt Schaafsma, for their lifelong rock art expertise; and the American Rock Art Research Association for their dedication to understanding and protecting this irreplaceable legacy.

Finally, thanks to Navajo Medicine Man Tom Tso; patient Marjorie Thomas; assistants Bobby Nez, Dennis Deswood, Jr., Leon Skyhorse Thomas, Daniel Staley and Mecinda for allowing us to record their sacred healing ceremony at Chinle, Arizona *(pages 16–19)*. Thanks also to Tom Tso's wife Connie Tso, their daughter Nancy Nez and grandson Gilmer Yazzie for their generous information and participation.

Introduction

America's dry southwestern climate preserves untold numbers of rock art sites within its far-flung network of canyons, cliffs and caves. It's a poetic domain of holy people and ceremonies in a magical land of earth and sky. The Native art in this booklet ranges from America's oldest (10,500–14,800 years old) to a recent Navajo sand-painting created and then ritually destroyed as a necessary part of a healing ceremony in 1993.

My painter-wife, Erma Martin Yost, and I were struck by the beauty of this rugged region when we first visited in 1976 and now, after four decades, we continue to return whenever we can. We typically fly to Albuquerque, Grand Junction or Las Vegas and then point our rental car in the direction of the Four Corners, taking in the wide vistas so opposite of our eastern home. We follow the trail of the rock art and talk with locals, gaining a sense of understanding while making new discoveries. We know we will never see *all* the rock art or its secret canyon repositories but each site we visit offers its own clues to the riddles left by the first Americans.

This booklet is a collection of images and stories gathered from 40-years walking, observing and photographing.

One Small Step

Pigment print
26 x 22 inches, 2013

These ancient Anasazi steps scale the precarious western edge of Comb Ridge in southeastern Utah. Deeply worn and weathered for more than 2,000 years, they still guide you quickly to safer ground. That's fortunate for the photographer because the late day sun doesn't wait for slow descenders. It's two photos—the top half is later in the evening a few miles away.

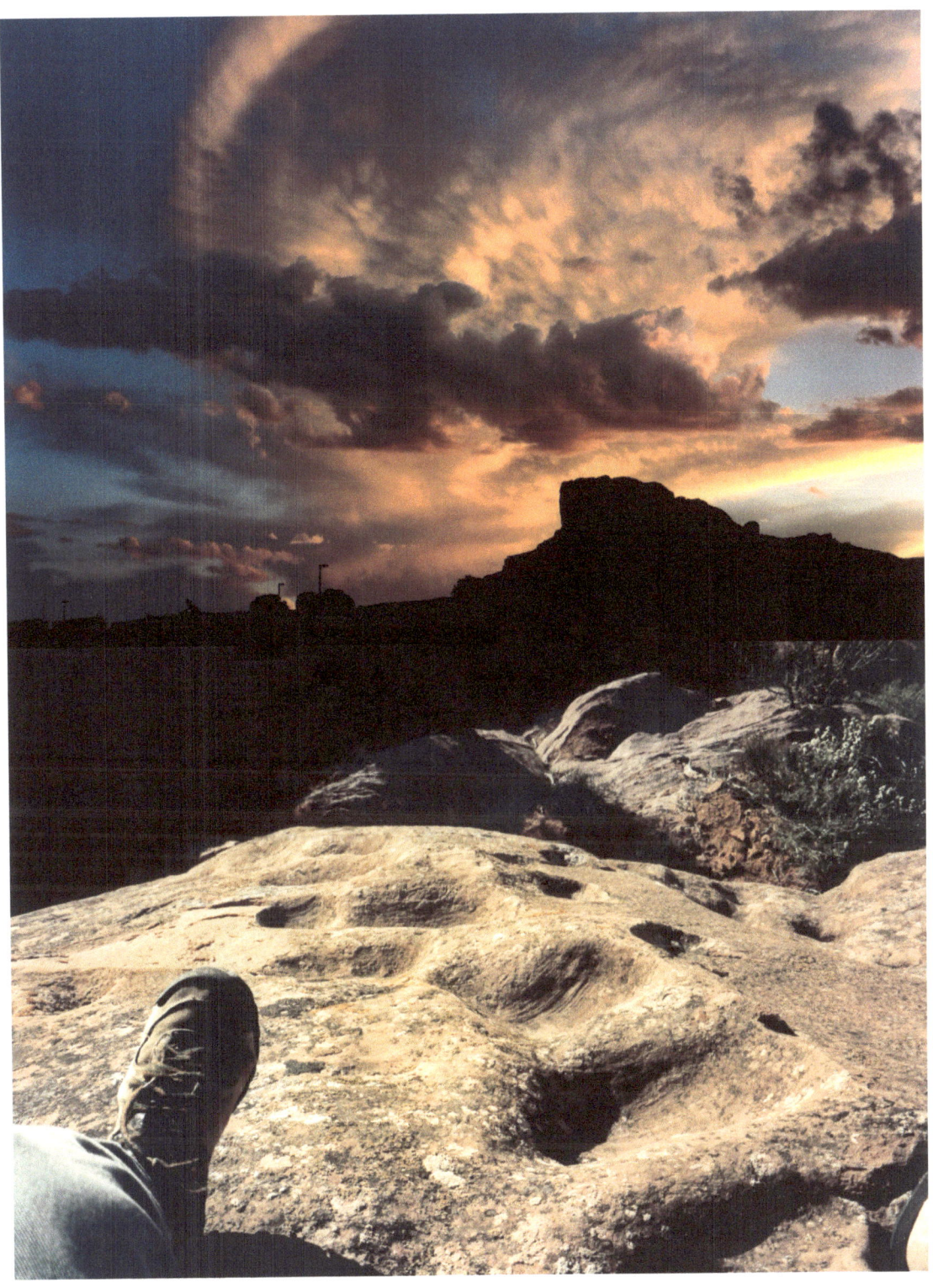

Procession Place
Pigment print
26 x 22 inches, 2013

Images on the rocks and the people who created them are a primary reason Erma and I go to the Southwest every year. We see the canyons as outdoor museums without labels. This mural in southeastern Utah was created about 1,000 years before Columbus discovered America. It depicts 147 little humans in a long crooked line above sheep with zigzag horns and tails. The lighter abraded spots likely resulted from medicine men harvesting rock substance to use in sacred ceremonies.

(lower right) This view is from the top of Comb Ridge where *Procession Place* is located. The ancient steps *(page 7)* lead up to this site.

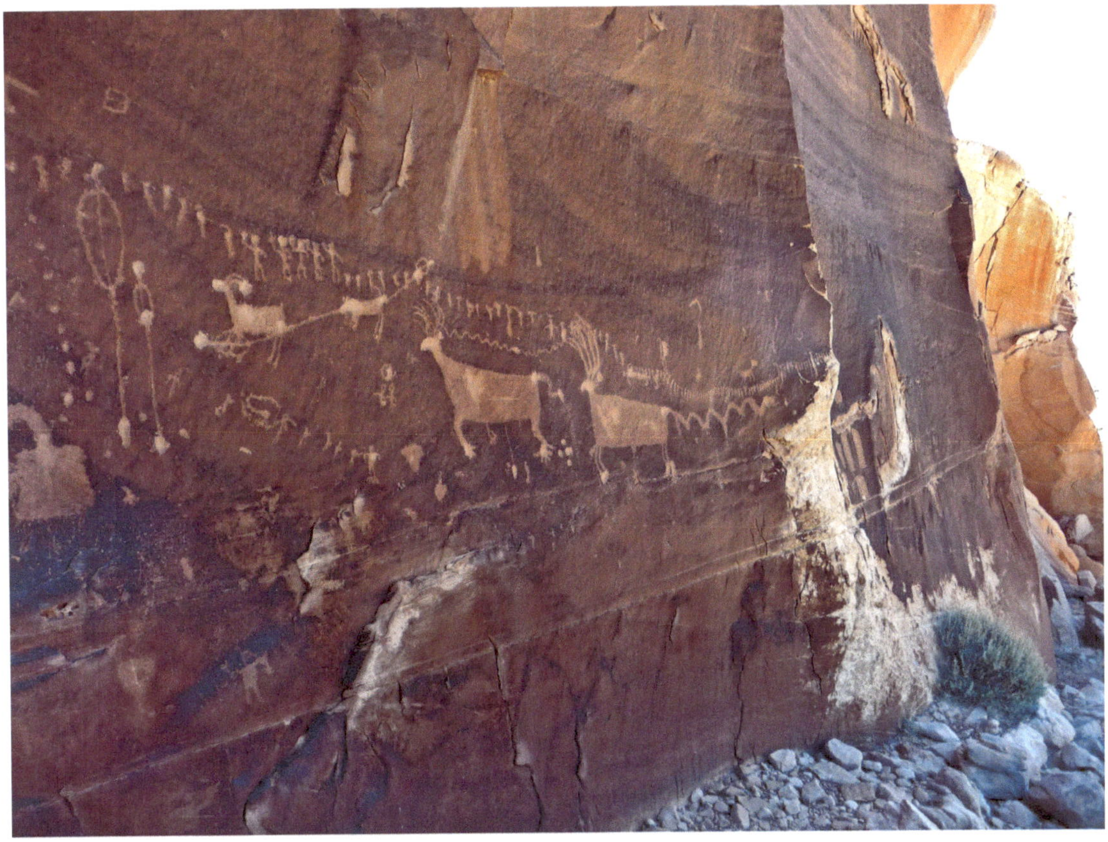

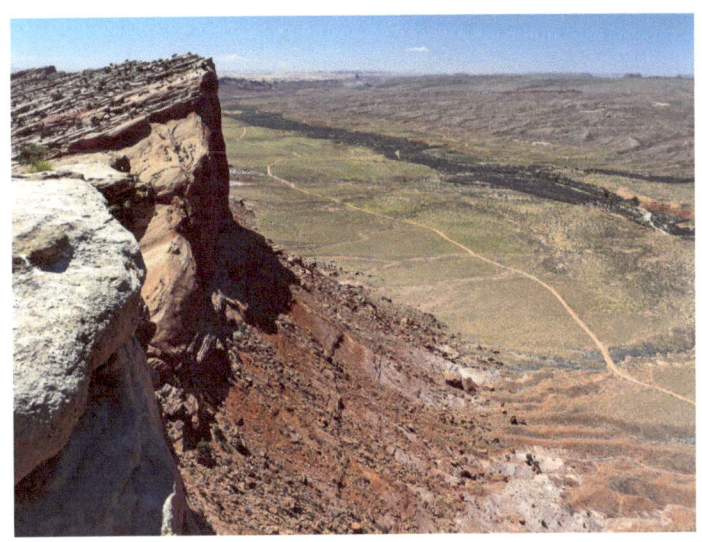

Hopi Villages of Second Mesa

Pigment print
26 x 22 inches, 2013

August 1976: Erma and I took our first trip to the American Southwest. She was an abstract painter and I was a photographer. We headed west from Albuquerque on the interstate with our eyes glued to the horizon looking for snowcapped mountains. I had promised Erma we would see some and a day later, even though it had been a dry winter, we caught a glimpse of the shining San Francisco Peaks silently rising in the distance. We popped our tent at Gallup, Flagstaff, and the south rim of the Grand Canyon and then on a Saturday morning headed northeast through the Painted Desert toward the three Hopi mesas. We were meeting two Anglo friends at a ceremonial Hopi Snake Dance, performed every other summer to bring the rain. This was not a show for tourists, but an actual sacred rite using live poisonous rattlesnakes! Snake dances have been closed to non-Native Americans since the late 1970s and cameras were strictly forbidden even back then.

About two-dozen Hopi men emerged from an underground kiva near the plaza of the pueblo village, each carrying several live rattlesnakes in their hands. They released the snakes onto the ground and kept them corralled there while they danced, using feathers to gently direct them back when they tried to slither away. Hopi women sat in a circle surrounding the dance area, each with a bowl of cornmeal that they scattered at the appropriate times. All the while, the dancers chanted rhythmic melodic songs timed to their steps as their dance-line moved round and round within the circle.

Erma and I with our two Anglo friends and a small group of visitors climbed ladders to the flat roofs of the adobe pueblo dwellings surrounding the plaza to watch the ceremony. The sun was searing and we were glad to be out of reach of the rattlesnakes! After two hours of watching the hypnotic activity we hardly noticed that the sky had clouded over and by the time the dancers gathered up the rattlesnakes for release back into the desert it started to rain. We quickly climbed down the ladder and began fast-walking to the car but a summer downpour hit us before we got there! We still don't know whether the dance brought the rain or if it just happened to come at the right time but this was our introduction the Southwest and now—nearly 40-years later—we are still going back.

October 1985: *(upper right)* Barely visible at the top of this photograph are the Hopi pueblo villages crowning the cliffs of Second Mesa where we watched the Snake Dance in 1976. Built of local materials in the ancient pueblo style, they blend so naturally into their environment that it's easy to pass by without even realizing they're there. The origins of Native American pueblo architecture go back to the 8th century.

(lower right) Fred Geary painted these Hopi women at the Desert View Watchtower in 1932.

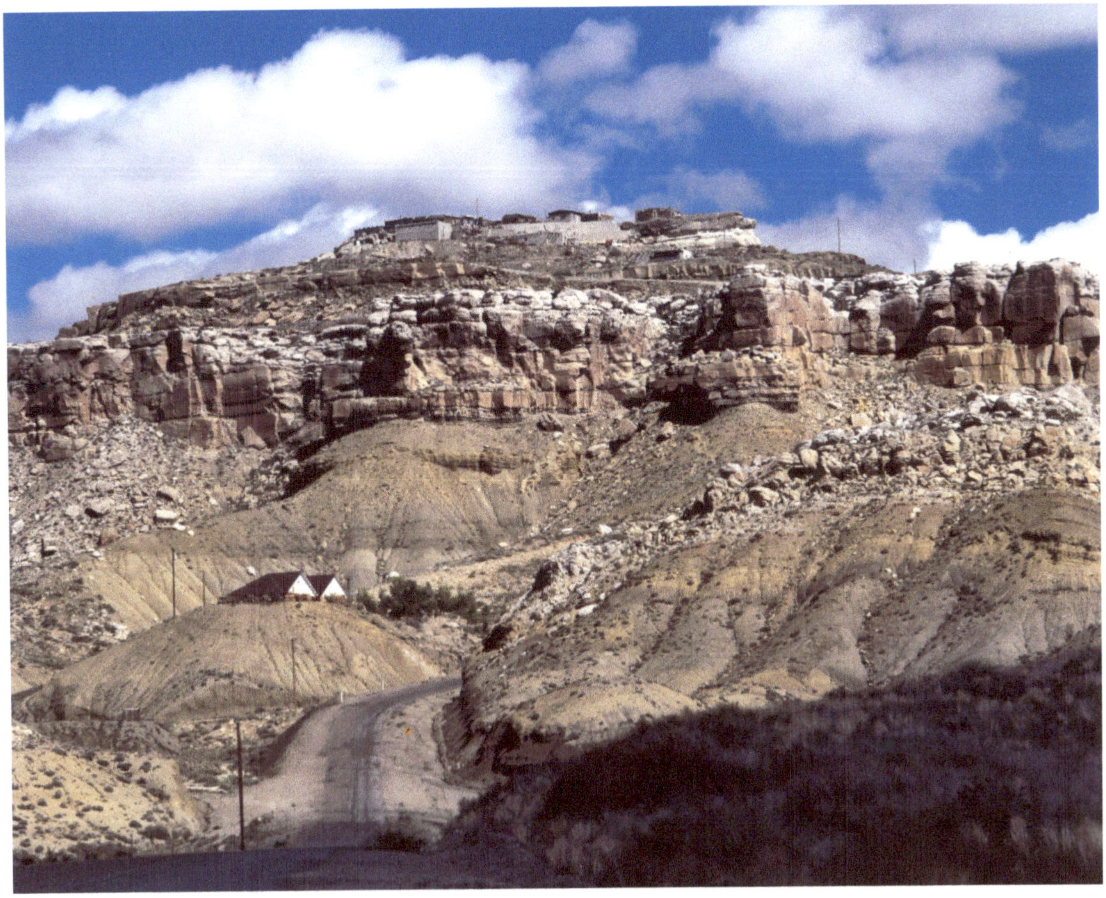

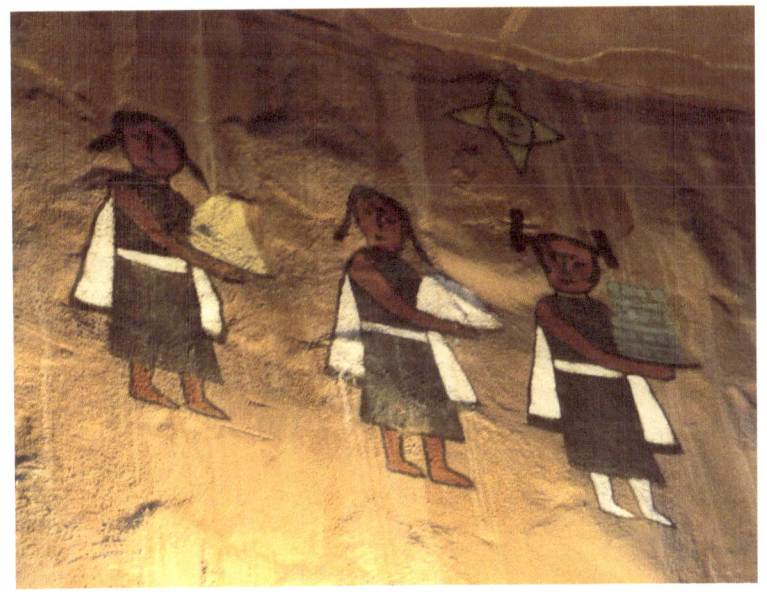

Desert View Watchtower

Pigment print
26 x 22 inches, 2013

June 2013: The sturdy stone Desert View Watchtower (1932) stands on the highest point of the south rim of the Grand Canyon. Its architect/designer, Mary Colter (1869–1958) was a strong-minded woman ahead of her time. Colter had traveled the Southwest working for the Fred Harvey Company and wanted this tower to fit naturally into its sublime surroundings, as did the 13th century pueblo observatories of Hovenweep and Mesa Verde that inspired her. Unintimidated by the male-dominated "modern" architectural world around her, Colter acquired major design commissions of her own for hotels and lodges along the Santa Fe Railroad including six in the Grand Canyon National Park, one of the Santa Fe's spur destinations.

A leader of the Pueblo Revival architectural style, Colter conceived of a tower that would grow organically from its setting. She employed Hopi Artists, Fred Kabotie and Chester Dennis along with Fred Harvey Company artist Fred Geary to decorate the interior walls with images from kivas and ancient caves.

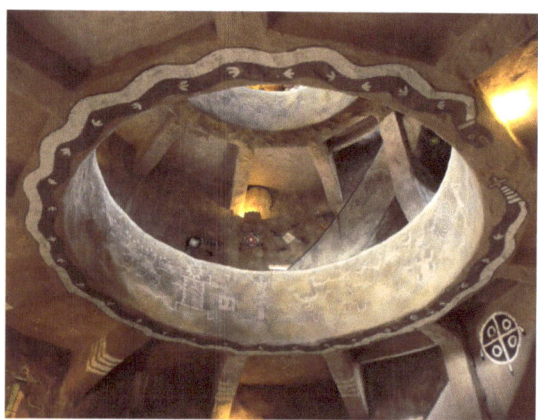

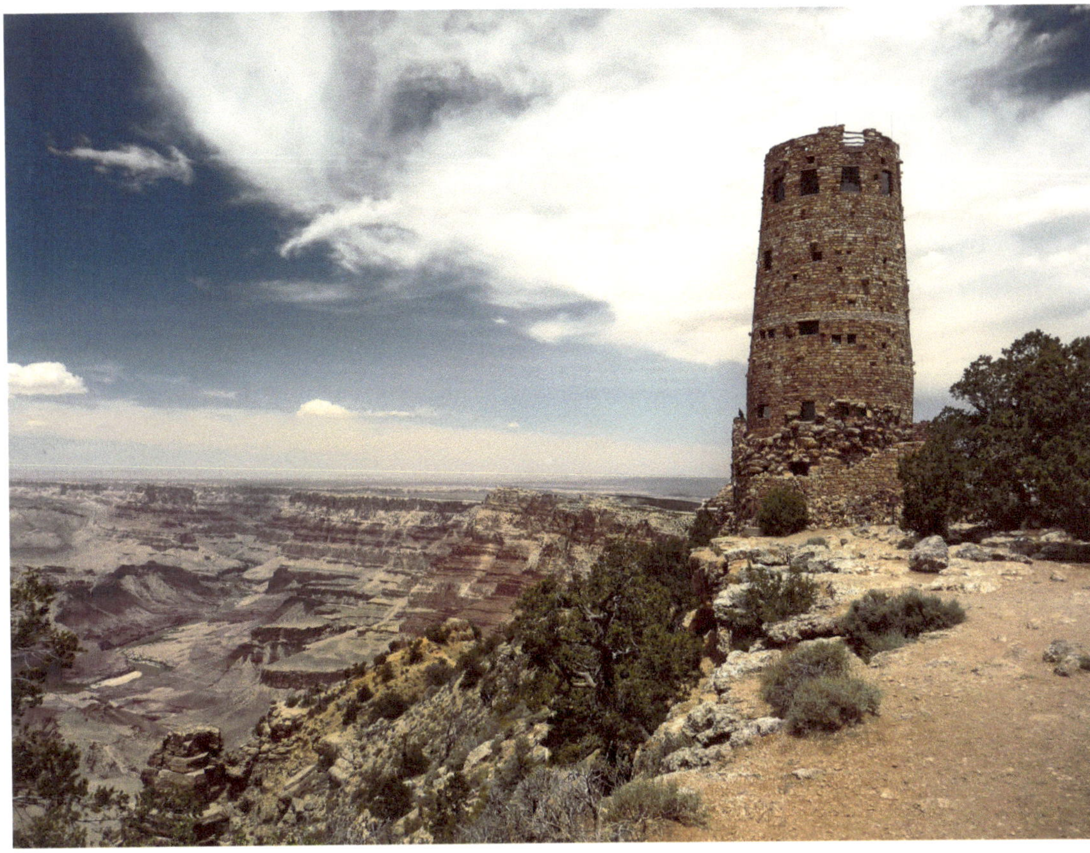

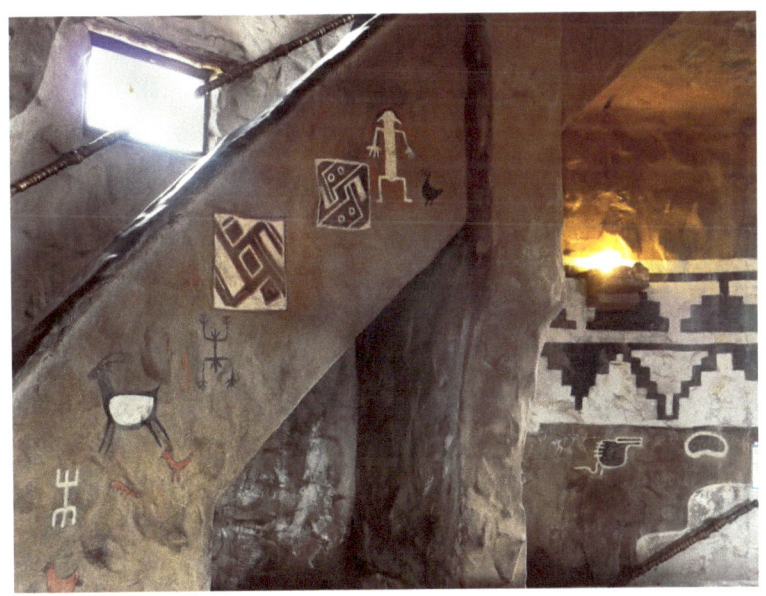

Navajo Basket-maker

Pigment print
26 x 22 inches, 2013

October 1993: *(upper right)* Connie Tso is a basket-maker, rug-weaver and wife of a medicine man from the picturesque valley of Many Farms in the eastern part of the Navajo Nation. Erma and I first met her when we were working with the BBC at Canyon de Chelly filming Desmond Morris' six-part series entitled *The Human Animal.* Connie is weaving a ceremonial patterned basket made from split sumac sprouts dyed red and black, contrasting with the natural beige. A bright striped blanket covers the entrance to the traditional hogan, indicating that preparations are underway for a healing ceremony. Two days later, her husband would begin the two-day medicineway at the patient's own hogan near Chinle, a few miles away. Connie was an active 69 years old in this photograph and when we revisited her and daughter and grandkids in 2012 she hadn't slowed much—at 89 years old.

March 1999: *(lower right)* This natural arch graces Connie Tso's "backyard" in Many Farms.

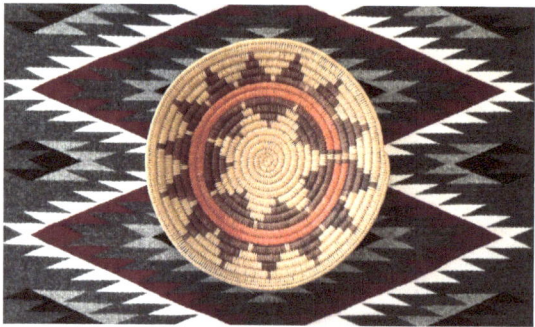

(above) Medicine men use Wedding Baskets to hold cornmeal and pollen during their ceremonies. The baskets symbolize the circular hogan and Mother Earth, their designs having an opening intended to be pointed toward the sunrise.

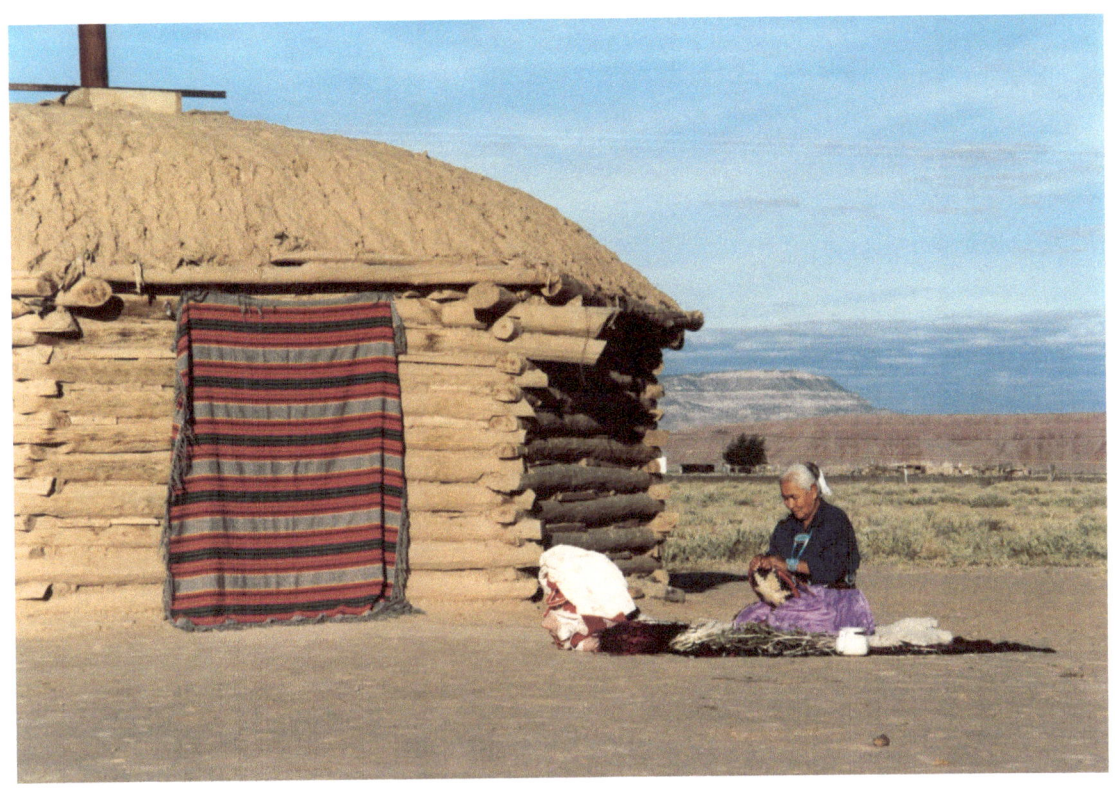

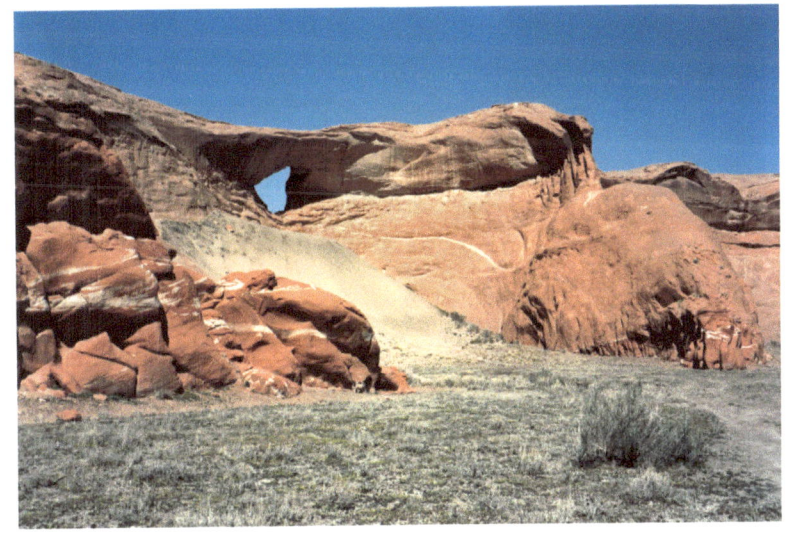

Morning Medicine

Pigment print
26 x 22 inches, 2013

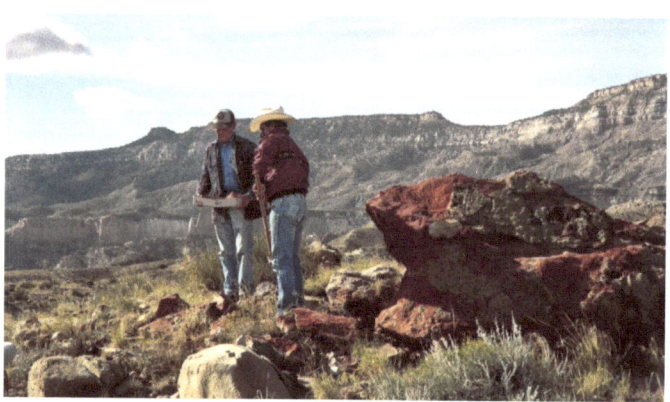

October 1993: *(lower right)* Medicine Man Tom Tso and five assistants created this sand painting the first day of a two-day *Red Ant Medicineway—Wolachii'ji* healing ceremony. It was made of finely ground sand from five colors of mineral-rock carefully trickled onto the earthen floor of the patient's hogan near the south rim of Canyon de Chelly. Tom Tso laid out the design and his assistants followed his directions to complete the necessary elements. To be effective for healing, certain parts had to be drawn to exact specifications while other decorative elements (like the kilts on the deities) could be improvised.

Today's traditional Navajos consider it dangerous to make religious works like this in a permanent medium because the power they contain can cause trouble if a knowledgeable medicine person does not guard them. Early Navajos did sometimes carve them on the rocks *(pages 22–25)* but

this practice is thought to have been discontinued around A.D. 1750.

We asked Medicine Man Tso what the figures represent and through an interpreter he said they are "holy people—people of the rainbow." From left to right he said they are "man, woman, boy, girl." The long narrow figure wrapping the bottom and sides is a rainbow deity *(full view is on page 18).* The painting took between four and five hours to complete.

(above) At dawn, Medicine Man Tso and his assistant Bobby Nez gather red hematite to grind into fine sand for the painting.

March 2012: *(upper right)* Morning light warms the cliffs of Canyon de Chelly. Cottonwood trees get this wispy-white halo just before the green leaves sprout.

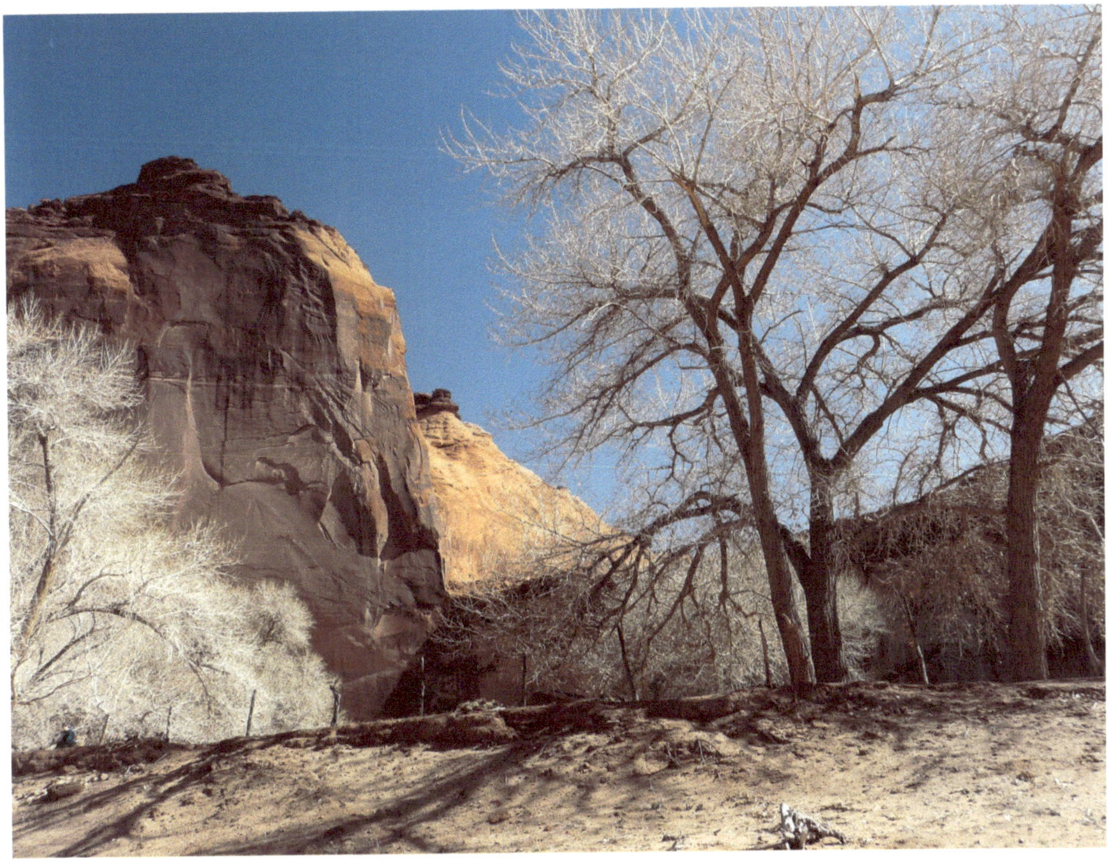

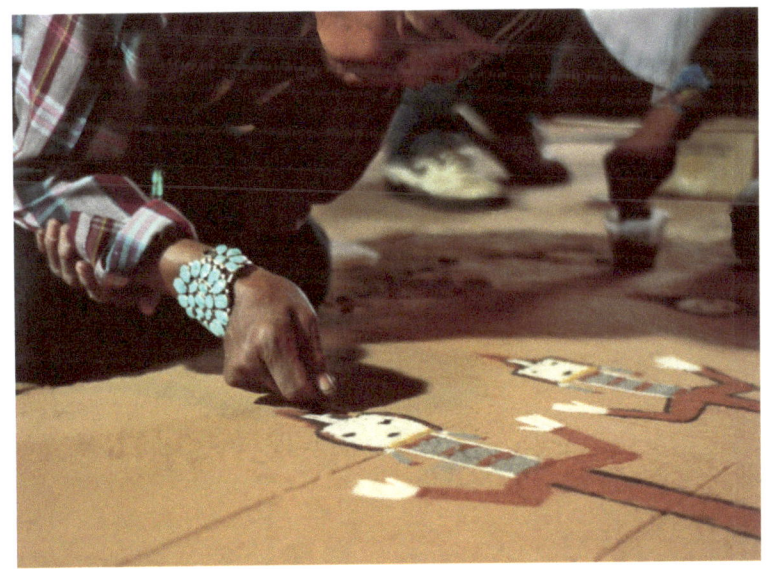

Navajo Healing Ceremony

Pigment print
26 x 22 inches

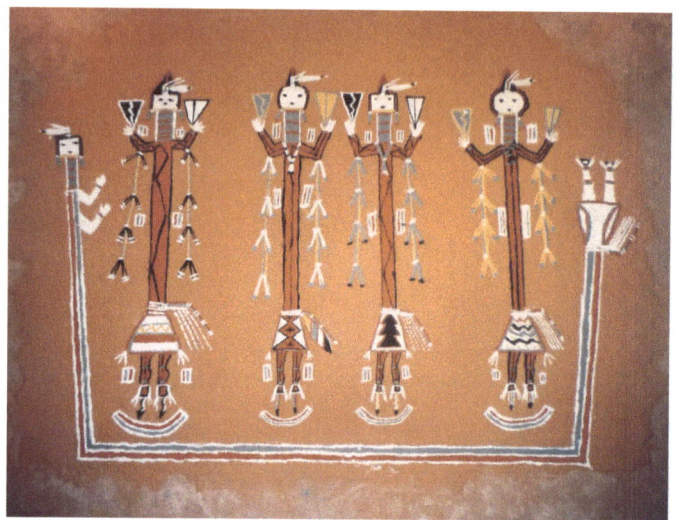

October 1993: (*above*) Once the sand painting is finished, the hogan is tidied up and the medicine man, patient, assistants, family, and invited guests all assemble inside. The medicine man rises to activate the deities, singing a chant while sprinkling the sand painting with cornmeal and pollen.

(*upper right*) Then the patient seats herself in the center and for about two hours the ceremony progresses with the medicine man and assistants singing chant after chant in unison, keeping time with a gourd and muffled drum. At the end, the patient rises allowing an assistant to sweep up the painting and carry it outside where he throws it to the wind.

Afterward, the patient may not work, bathe, or have sex for four days. There is no cooking, carrying water, doing chores, or going to a job. We were told, "she pretty much walks around and thinks about what has happened."

(*lower right*) After the ceremony, Medicine Man Tso gathers up his ceremonial tools.

Sincere thanks to Medicine Man Tom Tso; patient Marjorie Thomas; assistants Bobby Nez, Dennis Deswood, Jr., Leon Skyhorse Thomas, Daniel Staley and Mecinda. Also sincere thanks to Medicine Man Tso's wife Connie Tso, their daughter Nancy Nez and grandson Gilmer Yazzie.

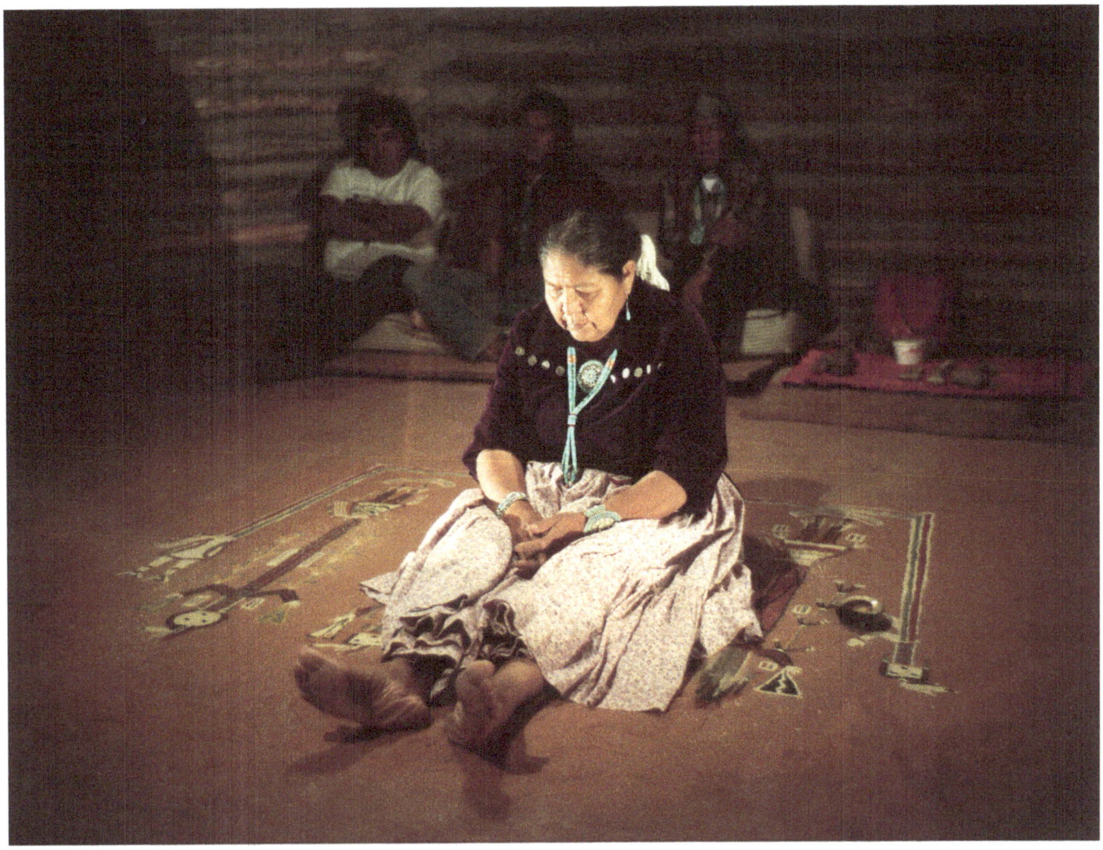

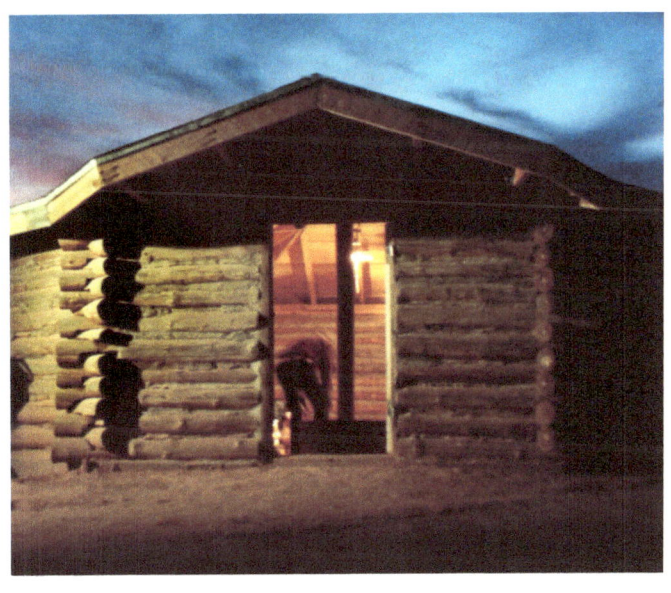

Restless Riders
Pigment print
26 x 22 inches, 2013

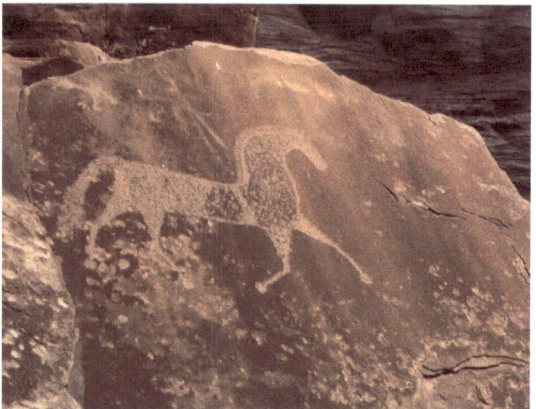

June 2013: *(upper right)* John Ford and John Wayne were here in 1939 filming "Stagecoach," the first of many westerns they made in Monument Valley. We could have rented horses from the Navajos just like they did but Erma and I decided to watch these tourist-riders from the sidelines. Scenes like this are the reason we like those old movies.

(above) Navajos quickly adopted horses from the Spaniards who brought them to North America. This Navajo-made trotting depiction is in Slim Canyon. It measures about one fourth life size.

(lower right) Hopi artist, Fred Kabotie painted this pictograph of a rattlesnake on the circular ceiling of the Desert View Watchtower at the Grand Canyon in 1932. Kabotie was sent to the Santa Fe Indian School when he was age 15 and while there he learned Anglo painting techniques but refused to unlearn his Hopi traditions. Intriguingly, in this image he turns the rattlesnake's usual forked tongue into a cross—a possible message to the Christians who attempted to convert him! The entire snake on site is 30-feet long. *(see page 12)*

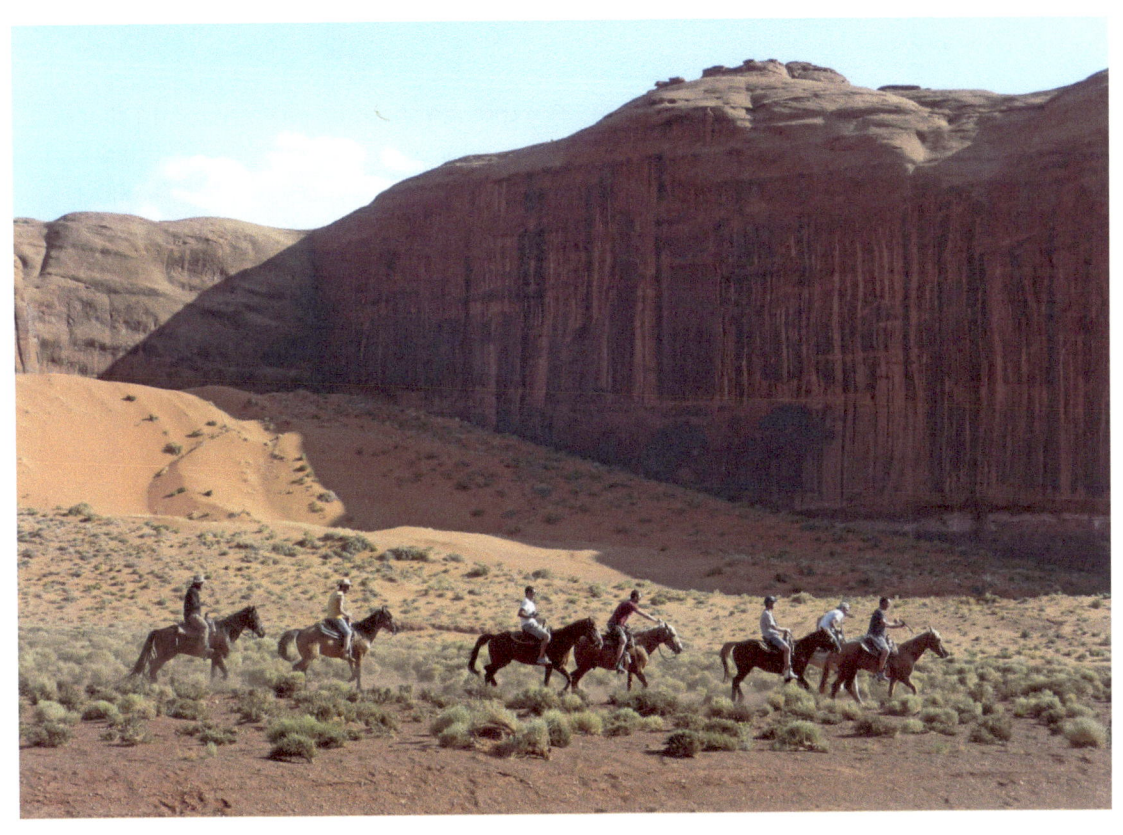

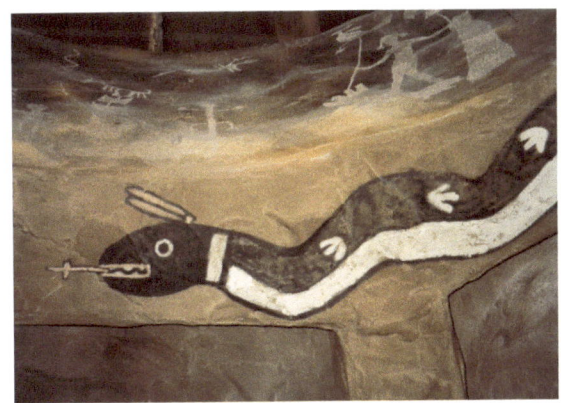

Bridge to Largo Canyon

Pigment print
26 x 22 inches, 2013

September 1996: "Five or fifty-five" was the advice the Bureau of Land Management archeologist gave before sending us off on the clay washboard road toward the low canyons of the Navajo ancestral land in northwestern New Mexico. *Dinetah* is the Navajo name for this terrain where they—*the Diné*—migrated from Alaska in the 15th century—about the same time Columbus was sailing toward America.

(lower right) This old steel bridge marks the beginning of a half-dozen or so miles of dusty road that leads to the mouths of three converging canyons that drain northward into the San Juan River. "You need to drive five or fifty-five," he said. "Five is slow enough to keep your bones from rattling and fifty-five is fast enough to skim the ruts." We drove five on our way in and fifty-five on the way out.

(upper right) We located the confluence of converging canyons using the hand-drawn map the archaeologist gave us and after crossing a wide sandy wash and bushwhacking through prickly brush we found the first of several petroglyph panels he had marked. The glyphs were close to the ground and the warm-toned morning light was good, so I was able to make sharp exposures of this intriguing mural depicting the horned Navajo harvest deity, *Ghaan'ask'idii.* This is one of sixteen gods and goddesses impersonated by actors in the nine-day *Nightway* healing ceremony that is still practiced today. The ceremony reenacts events from the Navajo creation story and elicits protective powers from the creators. Held after the first frost in the fall, it is elaborate, expensive and well attended. Typically hundreds of Navajos arrive for the mesmerizing public dance on the final night. Performed around four large bonfires, this *Yeibichai* (grandfather god) dance continues through the entire night from dusk to dawn.

(below) Red, white and ocher dancers grace a small shelter in a nearby drainage. They are not as boldly depicted as the petroglyphs, but their fragile beauty still stands the test of time.

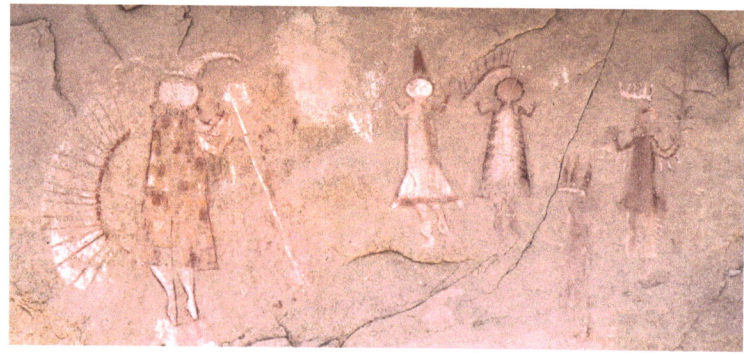

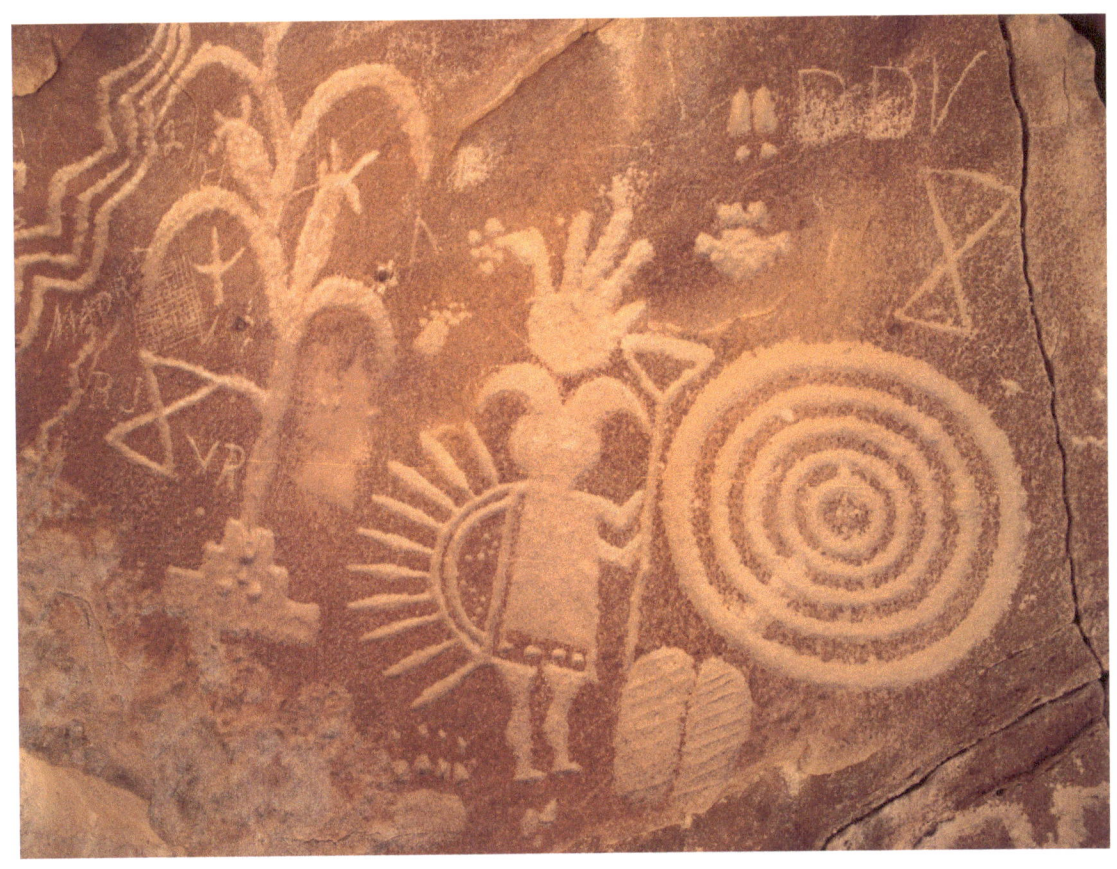

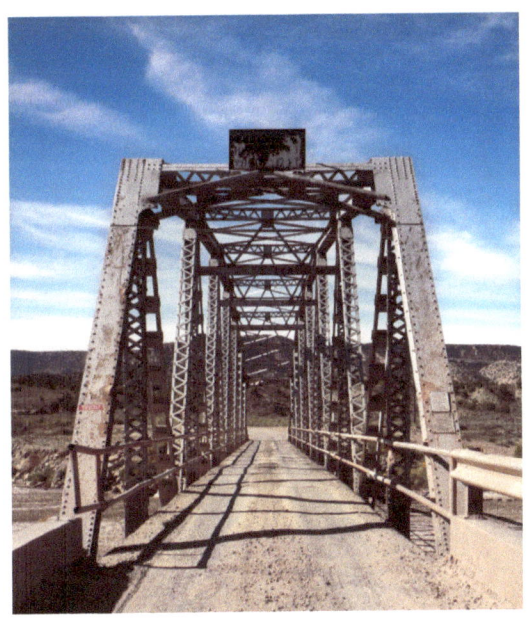

Emerald Crescent

Pigment print
26 x 22 inches, 2014

September 1996: *(upper right)* This petroglyph is carved with unusually fine precision into the sandstone wall of a small chamber of fallen rocks leaning against the red cliffs near the San Juan River. Well protected from wind, rain, and sun, there is little patina to differentiate the figure from the background making it barely distinguishable except when illuminated from a low side angle. Some 40-inches high overall (this is the upper half of the glyph) it depicts a Navajo deity, likely from the Nightway healing ceremony.

June 2013: *(lower right)* The San Juan River, framed in green, rounds a curve several miles downstream.

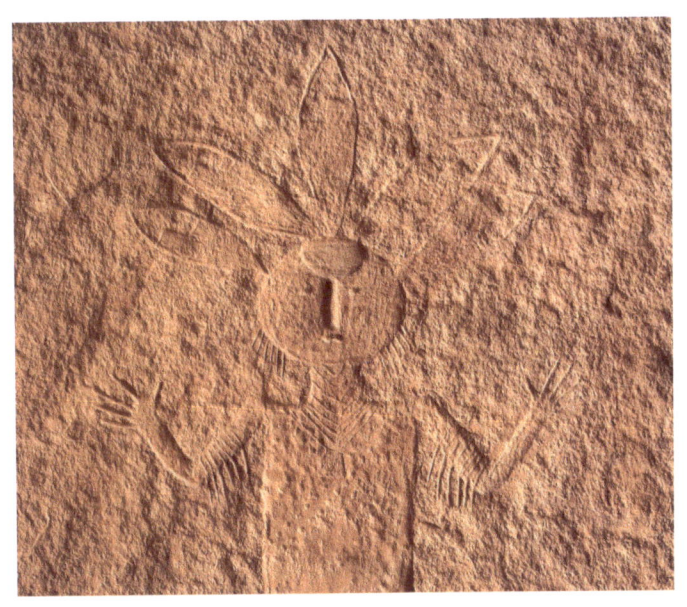

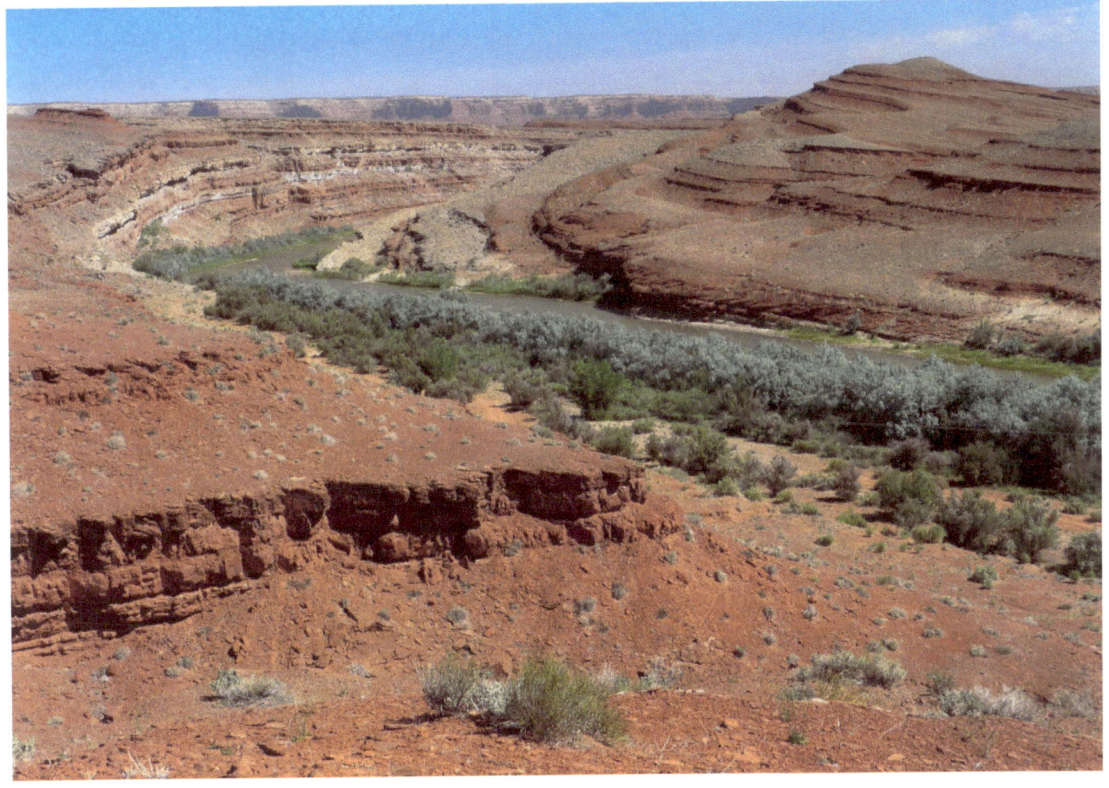

Crooked Road to Spirit Rock

Pigment print
26 x 22 inches, 2014

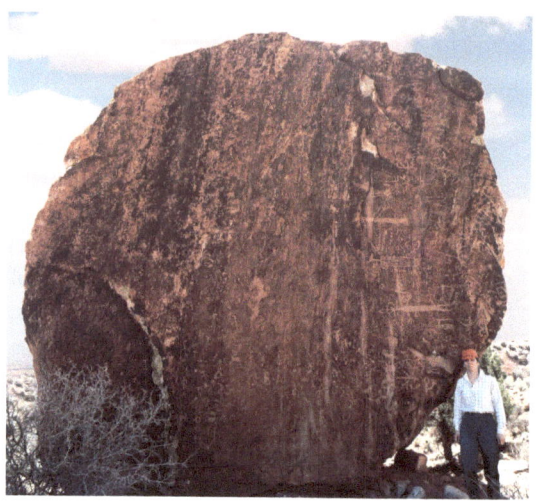

August 1977 was the first time Erma and I drove up the Moqui Dugway to Cedar Mesa. We had been camping at Monument Valley the night before when a dust storm blew a nasty piece of sand into my best eye. It felt like the eye was gone for good so at first light we rushed to the clinic at Gouldings and waited for it to open. The doctor on duty cleaned out the sand and taped up the eye—a procedure he was *very* experienced with—but my head was still throbbing and I was in no condition to drive the Volkswagen microbus. That's how Erma ended up in the driver's seat using a stick shift for the first time in her life.

June 1995: *(upper right)* The Moqui Dugway is a slippery gravel switchback road that climbs 1,100 feet up from the San Juan River bench - land in southeastern Utah. Countless cars have tumbled off of it over the years and some are still wedged between the rocks below because it's too difficult to winch them out of their vise-like crevices.

March 1990 and June 2013: *(above and lower right)* Millions of years of slow-but-persistent erosion have caused house-size boulders to tumble down 1,100-foot cliffs along the miles of meandering mesa-edge creating a jumbled world of sculpted stone. These petroglyphs are carved on one of those boulders. Some 2,000–4,000 years old, the glyphs likely depict ancient holy people. We can tell that the rock they are carved on has rolled within the last few thousand years because the figures are no longer upright. Now they are rotated 90-degrees sidewise, like a slow clock reading geologic time.

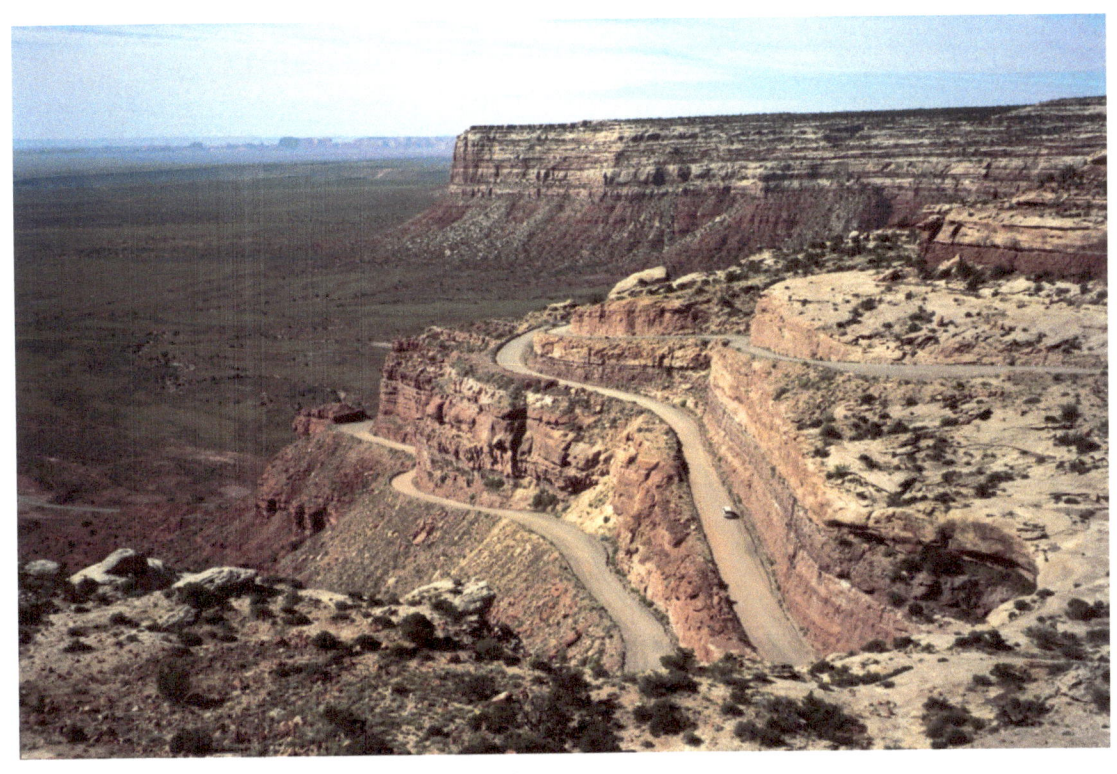

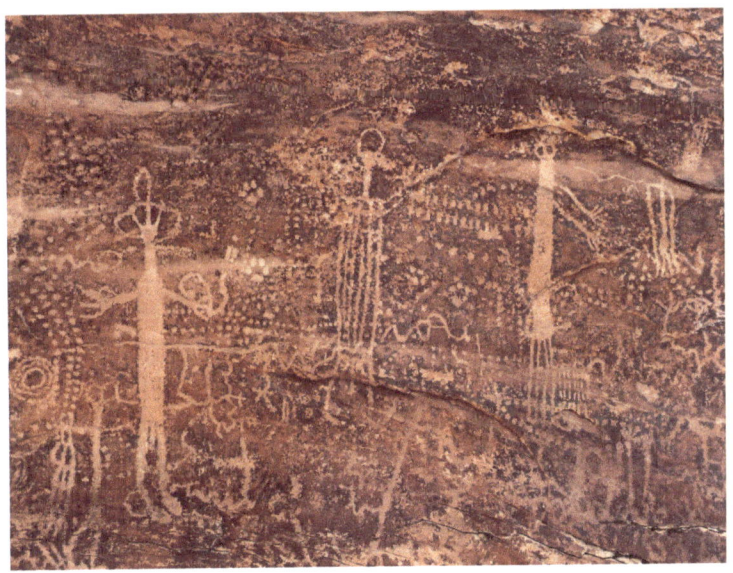

Medicine Mountain

Pigment print
26 x 22 inches, 2013

July 1998: The name "Temple Mountain" in Utah *(lower right)* sounds very Mormon, but Native American medicine men performed ceremonies at this natural shrine thousands of years before the first Europeans arrived. The rocky monolith thrusts upward through the San Rafael Swell in east central Utah. Its surrounding canyons preserve pictographs as many as six or more thousand years old. These are archaic Barrier Canyon style renderings of supernaturals, a style that until recently was thought to be one of the oldest in North America. (In 2013, some petroglyphs in Nevada were determined to be even older—10,500–14,800 years old—*see page 58*). Barrier Canyon style beings have elongated bodies with large eyes and small or absent feet. Supernaturals have no need for feet since they can move about at will without them.

(upper right) This intriguing scene is sheltered from the elements in a small alcove in a high sandstone bluff overlooking a broad canyon-riddled plain. A peculiar flying eagle (second figure from the left) features human-like legs attached to its posterior by a long crooked line. Hopefully the remote location of this fragile panel will offer some protection from 21st century humans!

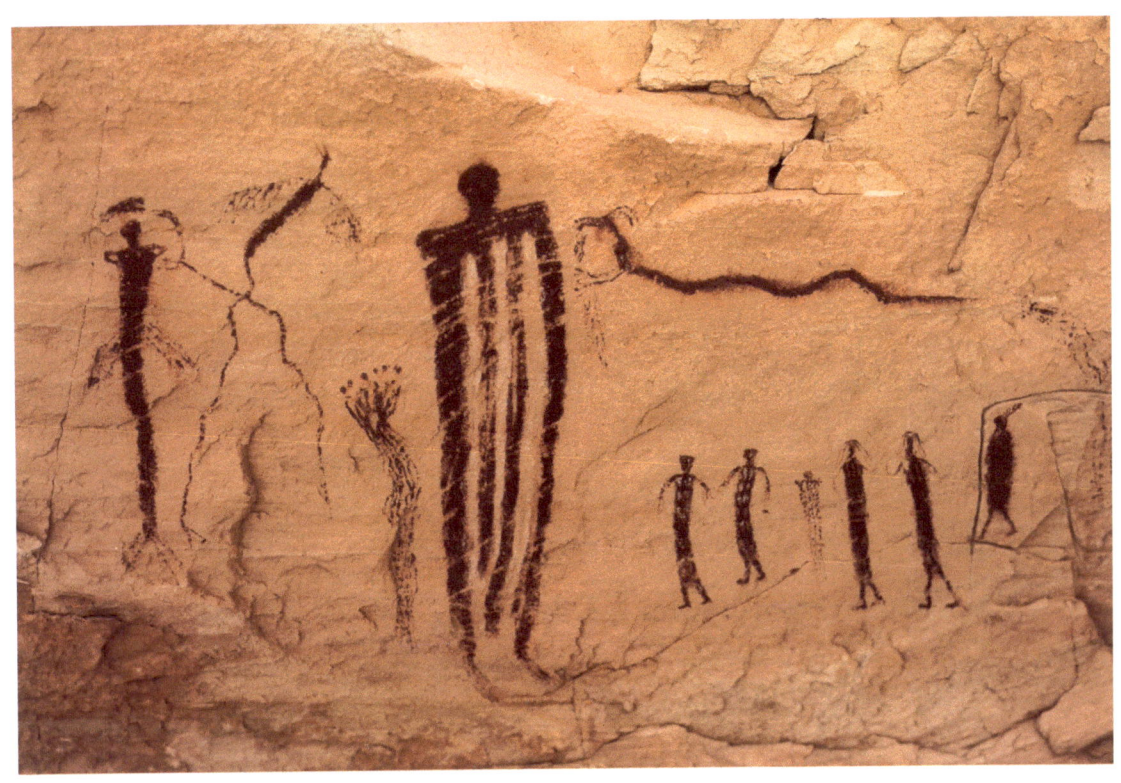

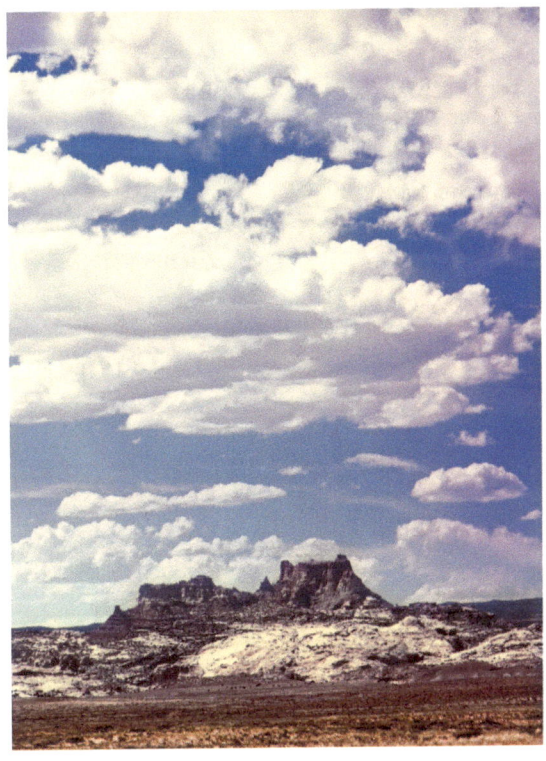

Shadow Spirits

Pigment print
26 x 22 inches, 2013

July 1964: The first time I stood on the rim of the Grand Canyon was on a much too fast summer trip during college. It was already dusk by the time our little group arrived at the rim, dumfounded by the vastness of the gaping chasm stretched out before us. When someone finally broke the spell, not a sound reflected back from the mile-deep, 18-mile-wide abyss. We stayed less than an hour because we needed to hurry back to Flagstaff to make our scheduled points west. I knew I had to return but didn't imagine that one day I would walk the unforgiving depths of the canyon's vast side tributaries looking for traces of ancient dwellers.

September 1998: Erma, two friends from Durango and I were up well before dawn, headed for the Arizona Strip, a triangular piece of rugged land north of the Grand Canyon and south of the Utah state line. It would be a long day, first on the backcountry Jeep-trail and then a backpack trek lugging lots of camera gear. We hiked a rugged and sometimes hard to follow foot-trail over lava flows 2,000 feet down into a wide multi-tiered tributary that drains into the Grand Canyon.

The usual way to find this remote pictograph site is via a three-day pack-animal trail but we opted for the faster more treacherous shortcut. Thanks to the topographical map a friend had marked up—and Erma's sharp eyes—we spotted the wide overhang filled wall to wall with pictographs as we rounded a bend in the sandy canyon floor.

(upper right) Crowded with life size anthropomorphic forms, some layered on top of others, the groups of "holy people" seem to pulsate, advancing from and receding into the warm-toned rock surface. Shown here is a detail (about five-feet wide) of the entire composition that extends some 40-feet along the chamber's back wall. It was likely created by generations of medicine men and women whose ceremonies and techniques were handed down from one generation to the next over their long habitation here some 2,000-4,000 years ago.

March 1982: *(lower right)* Erma rode the second mule up the South Kaibab trail. The rim was cold and snow-covered that day but deep in the canyon it was in the temperate 70s.

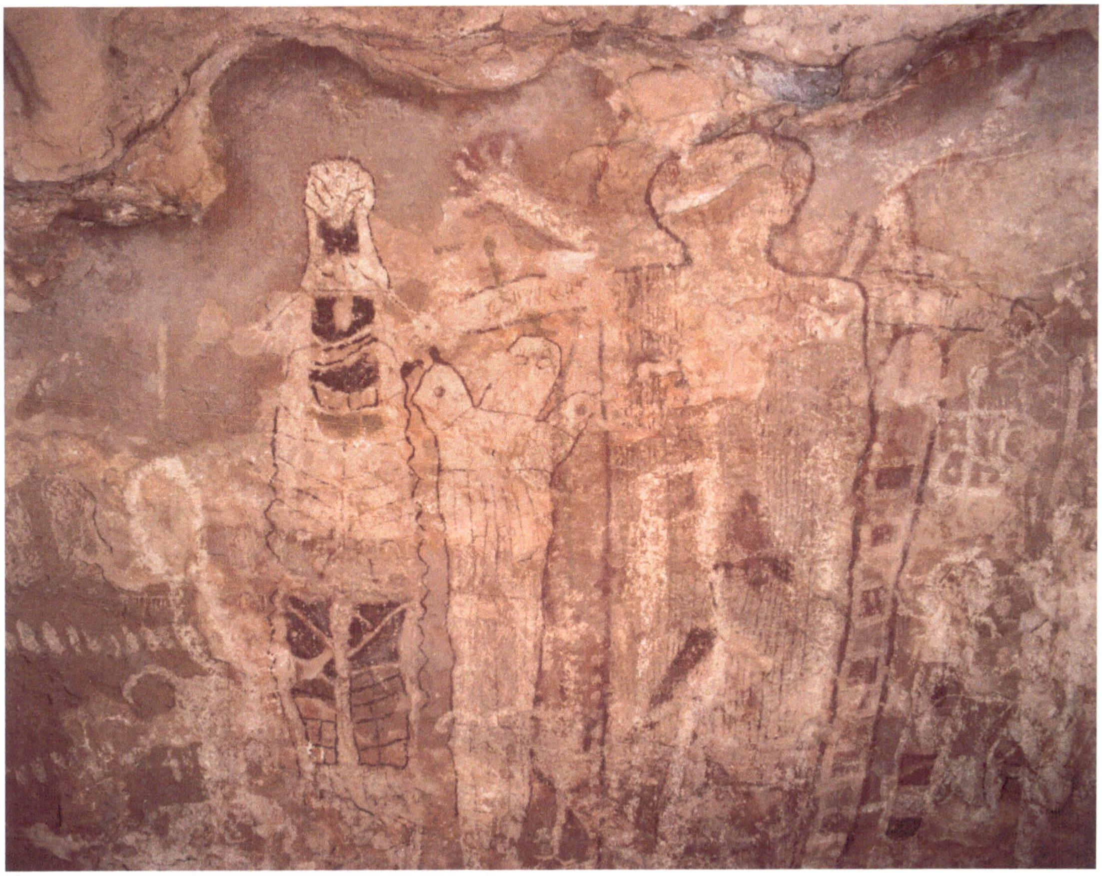

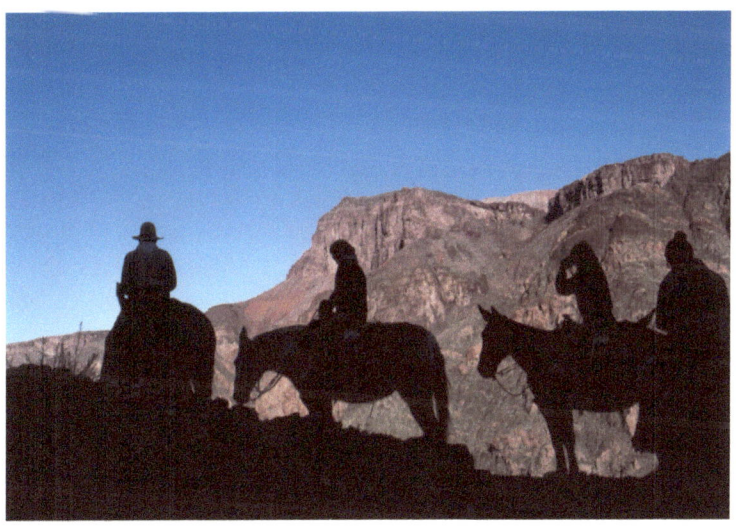

Lower Renegade Canyon

Pigment print
26 x 22 inches, 2013

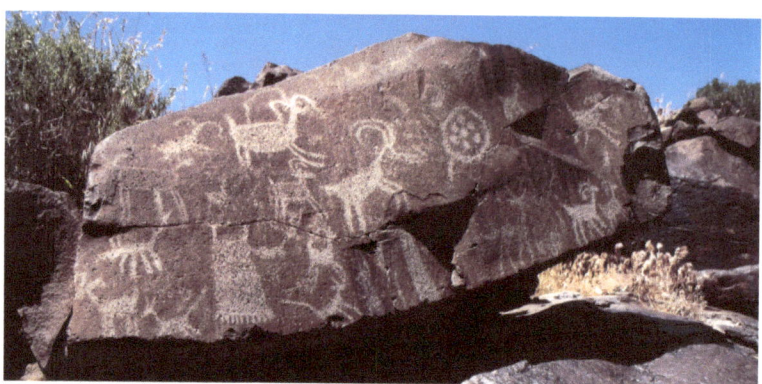

June 2009: The China Lake Naval Air Weapons Station in the Mojave Desert near Ridgecrest, California covers 19,600 square miles, an area larger than the state of Rhode Island. It's a test and research site with more than 2,000 miles of mostly gravel roads connecting its far-flung boundaries. In addition to military hardware, the Station encompasses the high canyons of the Coso Range, claimed to contain more than 50,000 petroglyphs. Lower Renegade Canyon has the highest concentration, so that is where Erma and I signed up to tour. The Navy tightly guards the area and limits canyon tours to allotted periods on the station's down days. After the inspectors had mirrored and sniffed our car and contents, we were given the green light along with several other vehicles led by the guide from the local museum. It was an hour's drive past a low dry lakebed, and then up through the foothills to the black basalt Renegade Canyon a mile above sea level.

As soon as we entered the sandy bottom of the rocky twisting canyon we were struck by the plethora of perfectly preserved images all around us. Ancient artisans had obsessively carved boulders and walls, revealing the light toned base-rock under the dense purple-black patina. Meandering abstracts and flocks of desert bighorns abounded, punctuated by humans with sunburst heads and decorated torsos. Some theorize that these may be shamans seeing to the survival of the flocks in the harsh environment. We saw the canyon as an immense art gallery, but we also know the Native Americans who created the images had no word for "art." To them, pictures on the rocks were made for function and sacred ceremonies.

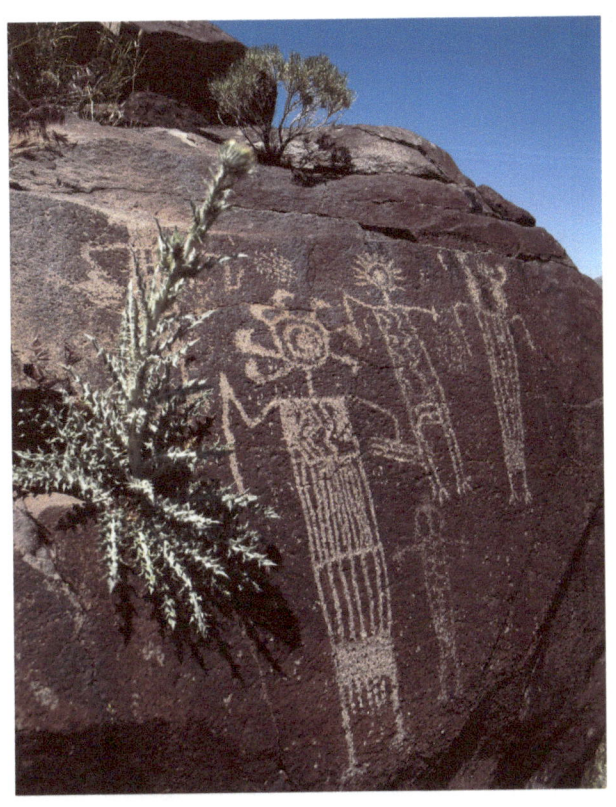

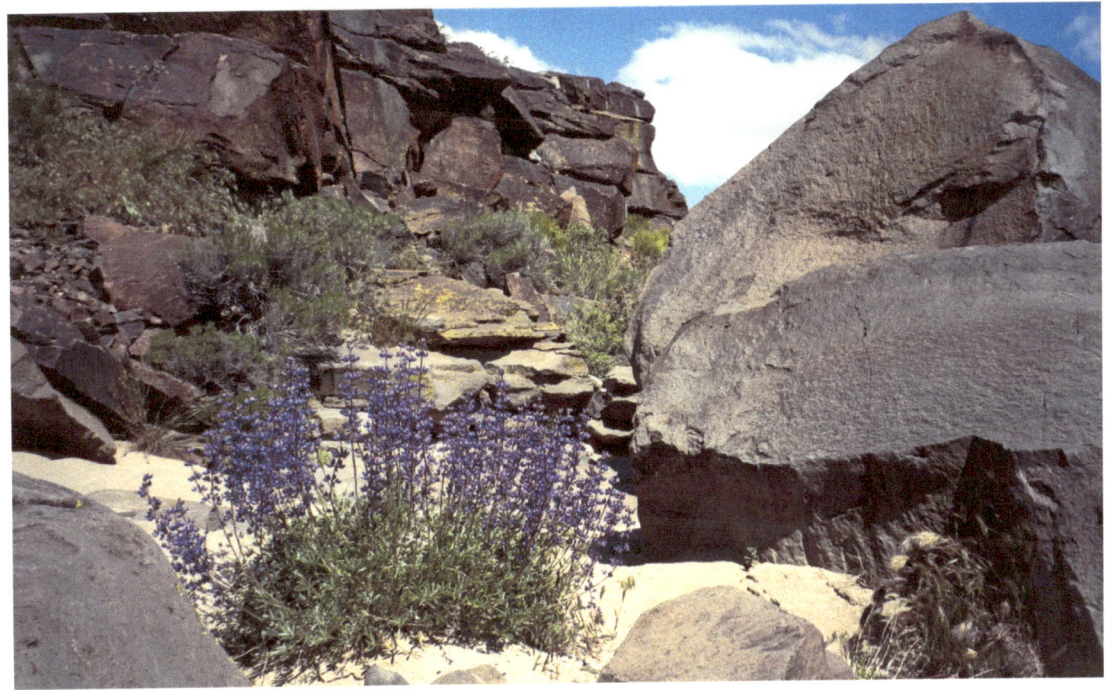

An Ancient Shrine

Pigment print
26 x 22 inches, 2013

January 1985: The last thing Erma and I expected to find when we started traveling to the southwest in the 1970s was a possible ancient temple in Utah's maze of meandering canyons. But that is what we discovered on New Year's Day 1985 when Wendy Quick, an Anglo friend from the area, guided us to this mysterious secluded site in the sweeping spaces stretching south from Price. Wendy led us down a crooked cow-path into a rocky ravine and from there we picked our way along an eons-old natural stone dyke toward a cluster of massive rectangular pillars rising from an island-like point of land. We had previously seen a photograph of an intriguing rock art mural located there and Wendy had offered to take us. We were prepared to see impressive rock art that day but not the profoundly powerful setting. There was too much for us to digest in one visit so we've returned to this natural shrine many times since.

Nature-based religions like the Native Americans' have no need to *build* sacred spaces. Rather, they seek out and appropriate those already existing in the environment. This site is still guarded today—and we've seen the evidence.

On our first visit, Erma found five rattlesnake skins on the trail and the following June she startled a long snake slithering across the trail where she was poised to plant her next step! I missed the moment because I was still at the car collecting camera gear and by the time I got there it was gone.

March 1991: *(lower right)* That's Erma posing at the summit of the "grand staircase" that leads to an upper section covered with flat-topped altar-like rock-forms. The petroglyph panel is on the right.

(upper right) A rainbow arcs over beasts, birds, serpents, humans, animal tracks, and abstractions, some superimposed and others connected by wavy lines. The lighter glyphs are most recent and the darker ones older, like a book reaching back through time. Utes made the newest images within the last few hundred years, but the archaic ones may date back as far as several thousand. The light-colored band across the top resulted from a misguided individual's attempt to pry off pieces of the panel sometime in the 20th century.

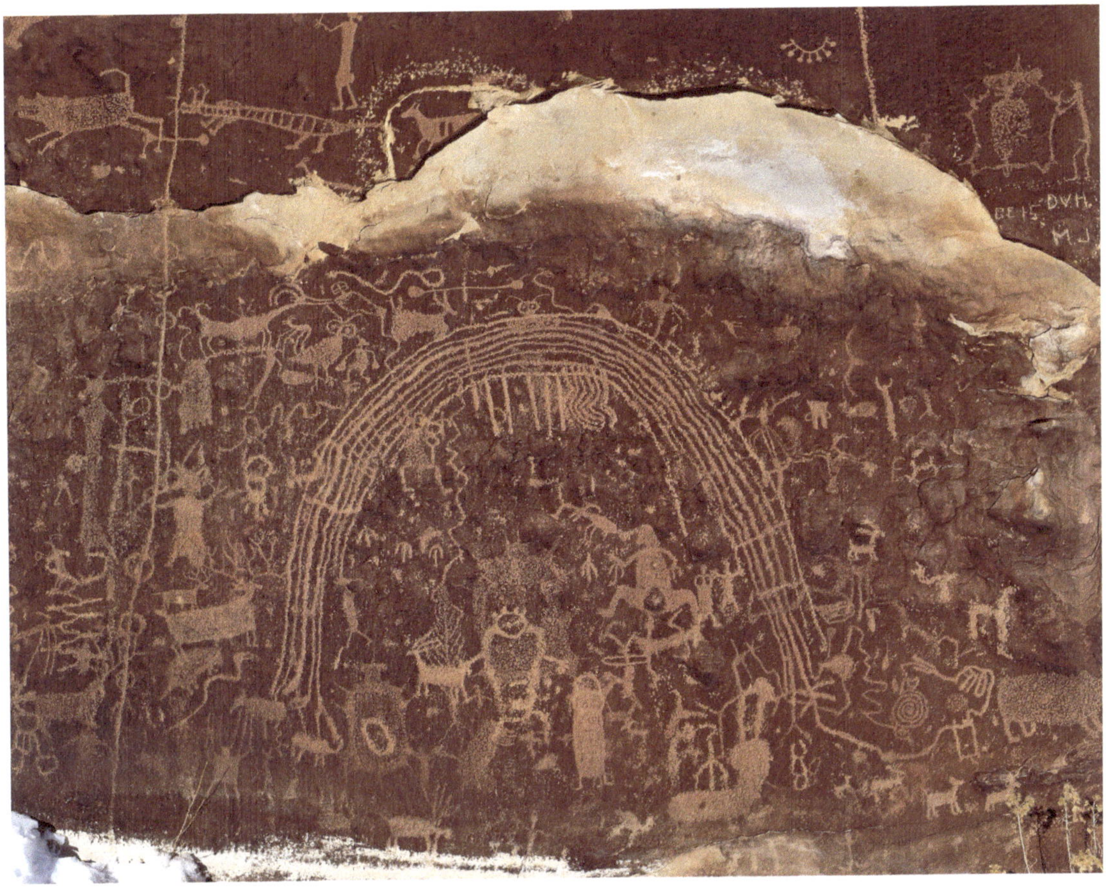

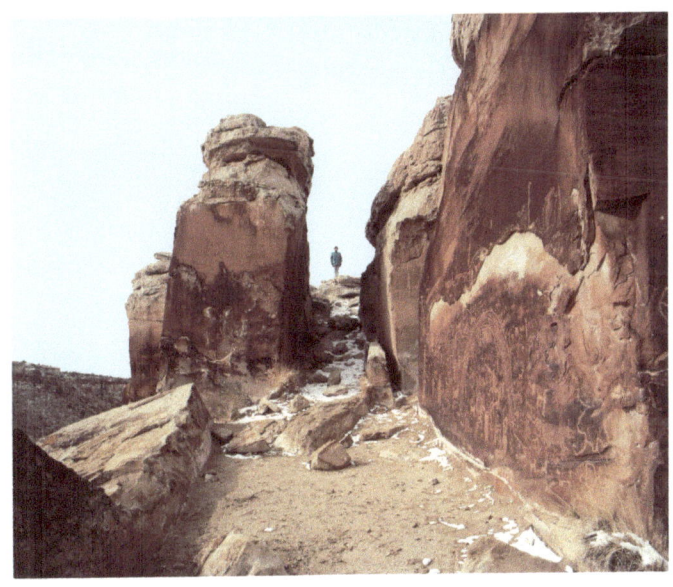

Land of the Eagle

Pigment print
26 x 22 inches, 2013

October 1994: *(below)* Eagle's Nest and Green Circles are two short steep finger-canyons that cut deeply into Comb Ridge, each rising some 800-feet toward a shared saw-tooth summit a mile or two from their mouths. An inaccessible Anasazi ruin is high in an alcove of Eagle's Nest—giving the canyon its name—and three large green and white concentric circles are painted on the steep walls of nearby Green Circles Canyon.

The Autumnal Equinox had just passed and Erma and I spent the afternoon watching a shadow creep to the center of the largest green and white circle, then pause there while the sun passed over the cliffs. We were watching the canyon function as a giant celestial calendar. We've been back several times during both the spring and autumnal equinoxes and to us the shadow-marker is very convincing.

(lower right) The day was late and we were hastily hiking out of the canyons when I stopped to capture this scene looking back across the slickrock. The shadows had transformed the eroded terrain into a seeming sea of giant turtles on an epic migration—a vivid illusion to tired hikers!

(upper right) Fred Geary painted this stylized eagle at the Desert View Watchtower in 1932.

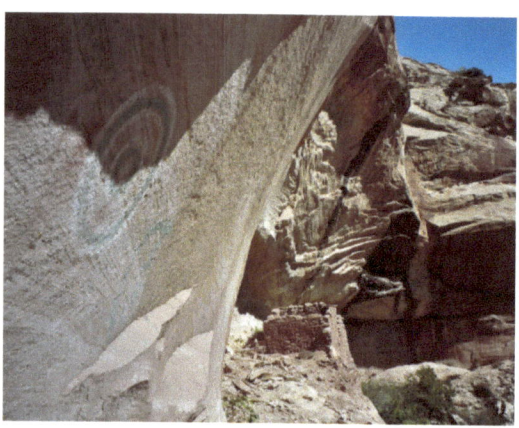

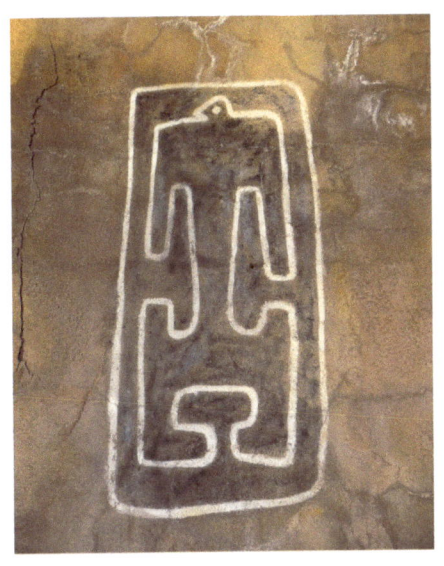

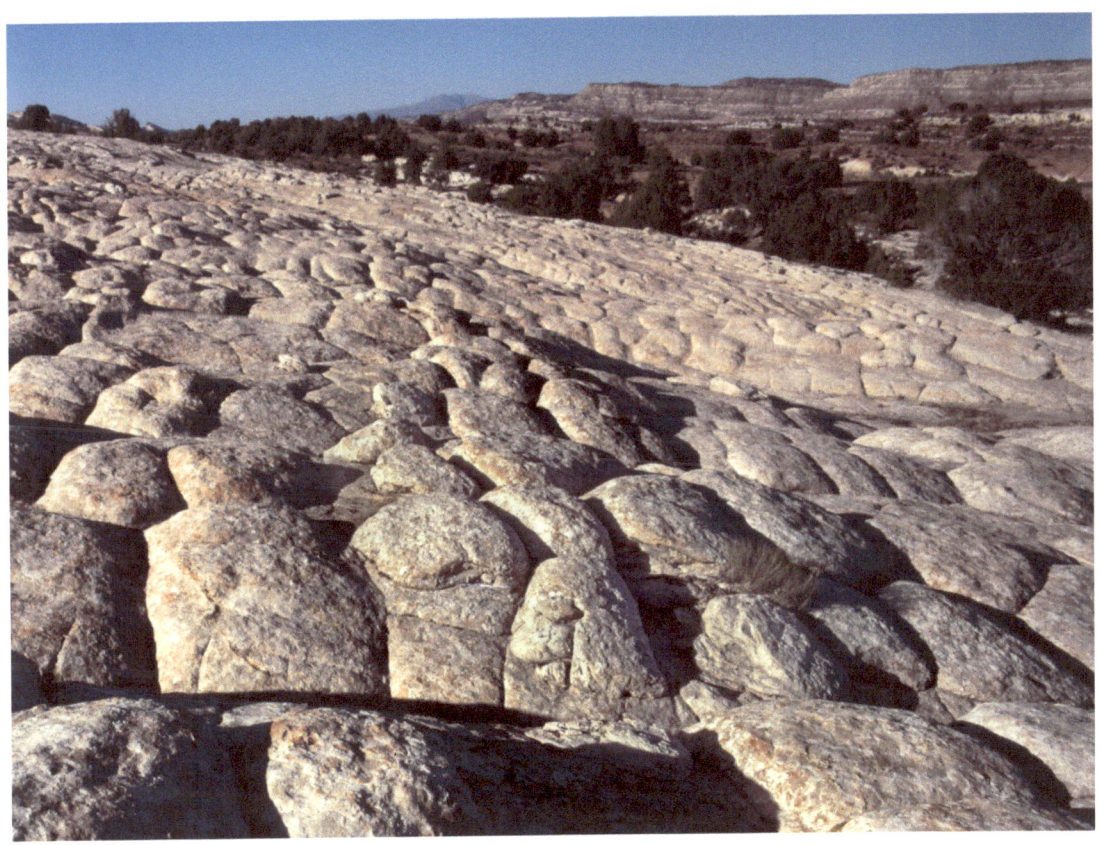

White House Revisited
Canyon de Chelly

Pigment print
28 x 20 inches, 2013

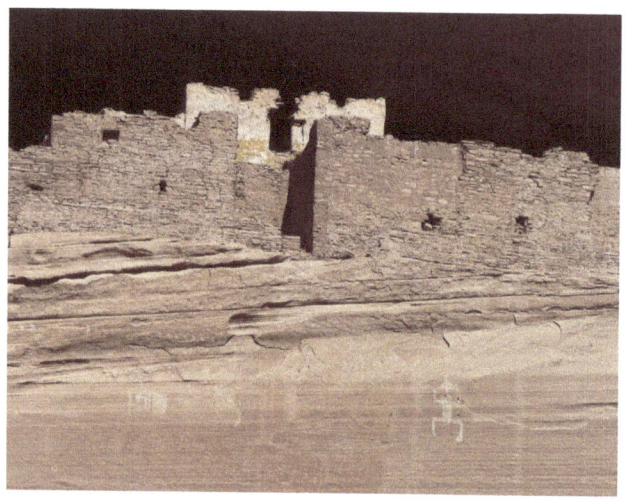

March 2012: *(above and upper right)* Ansel Adams made his famous large-format black and white image from this spot in Canyon de Chelly on an April afternoon in 1949. Sixty-three years later, Erma and I hiked the same trail on a March morning, capturing these views with a tiny digital camera—but the real drama in both cases was the canyon itself!

(lower right) Fred Geary painted these pictographs on a wall of the Desert View Watchtower in 1932. The white human figure may have been inspired by the similar figure seen faintly on the cliff-face of the above photograph *(just below the ruin)*.

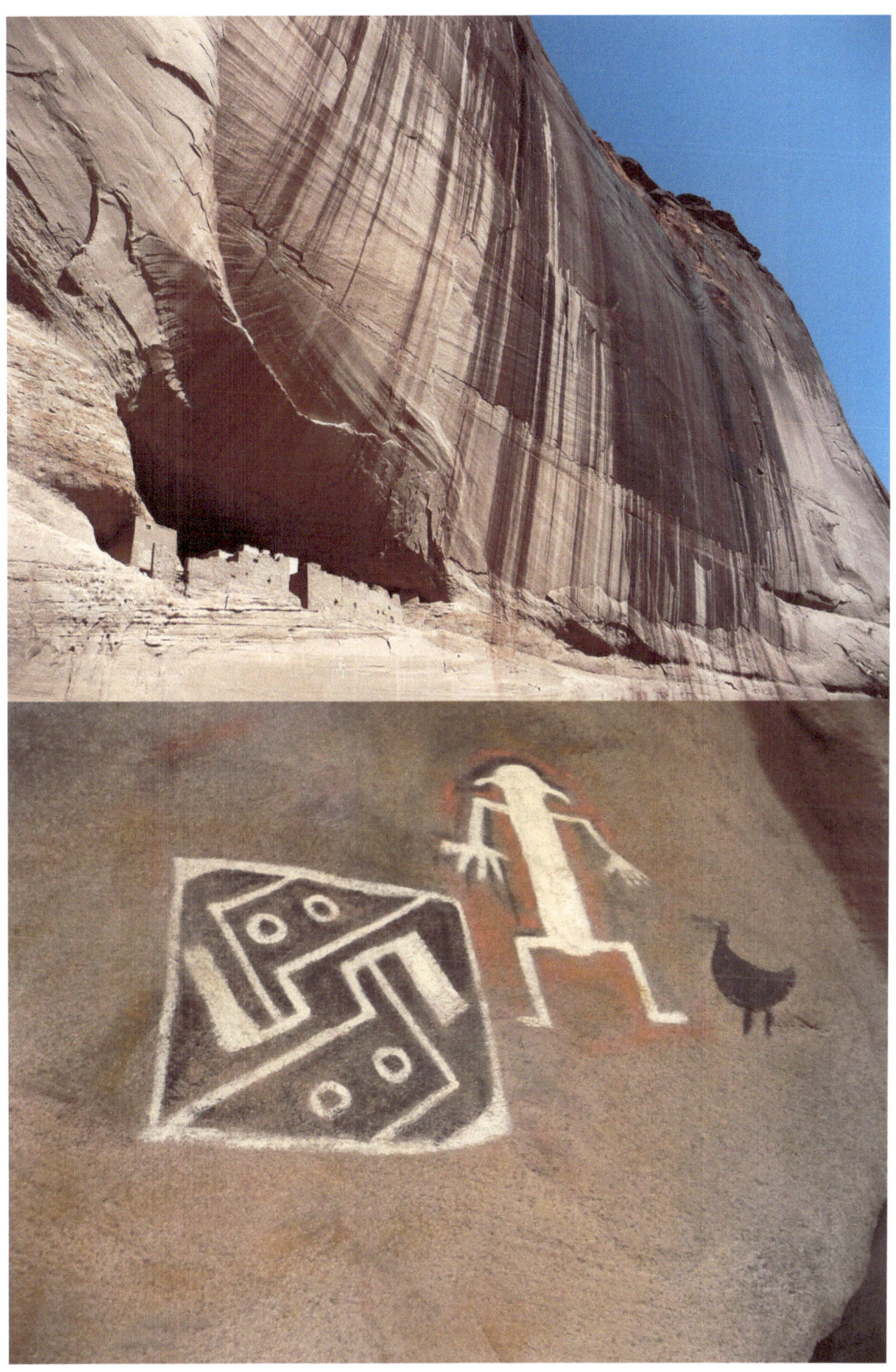

Rainmaker Cave

Pigment print
26 x 22 inches

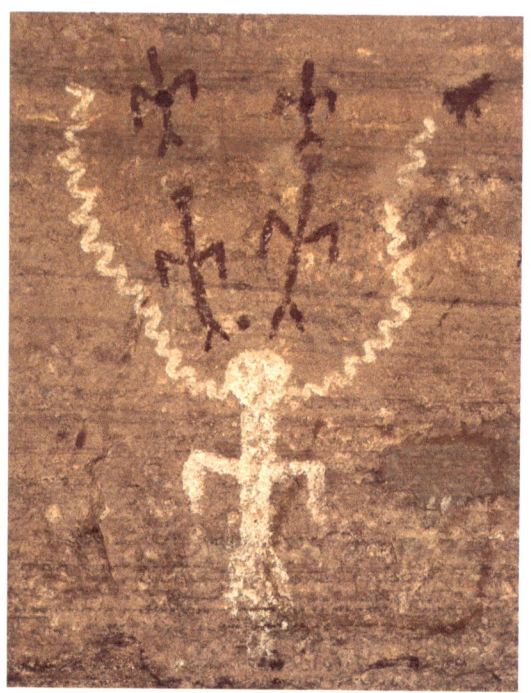

July 1986: Canyon de Chelly preserves a wealth of ancient culture including major Basketmaker art (300 B.C.–A.D. 800). Pictographs from this period are boldly painted with generous amounts of pigment and evocatively powerful designs.

(upper right) This composition is painted on the back wall of an alcove (aka Pictograph Cave) in a small side canyon not far from White House ruin. The red and white handprints give scale, indicating that the large white duck (outlined in amber) is about 32 inches long. Flute players are thought to have summoned rain and the pair under the duck feature rainbow halos, possibly indicating success.

(above) Headdresses symbolize power and this is one of the more elaborate in the area.

December 1984: *(lower right)* This view from the rim of the canyon is a short distance downstream.

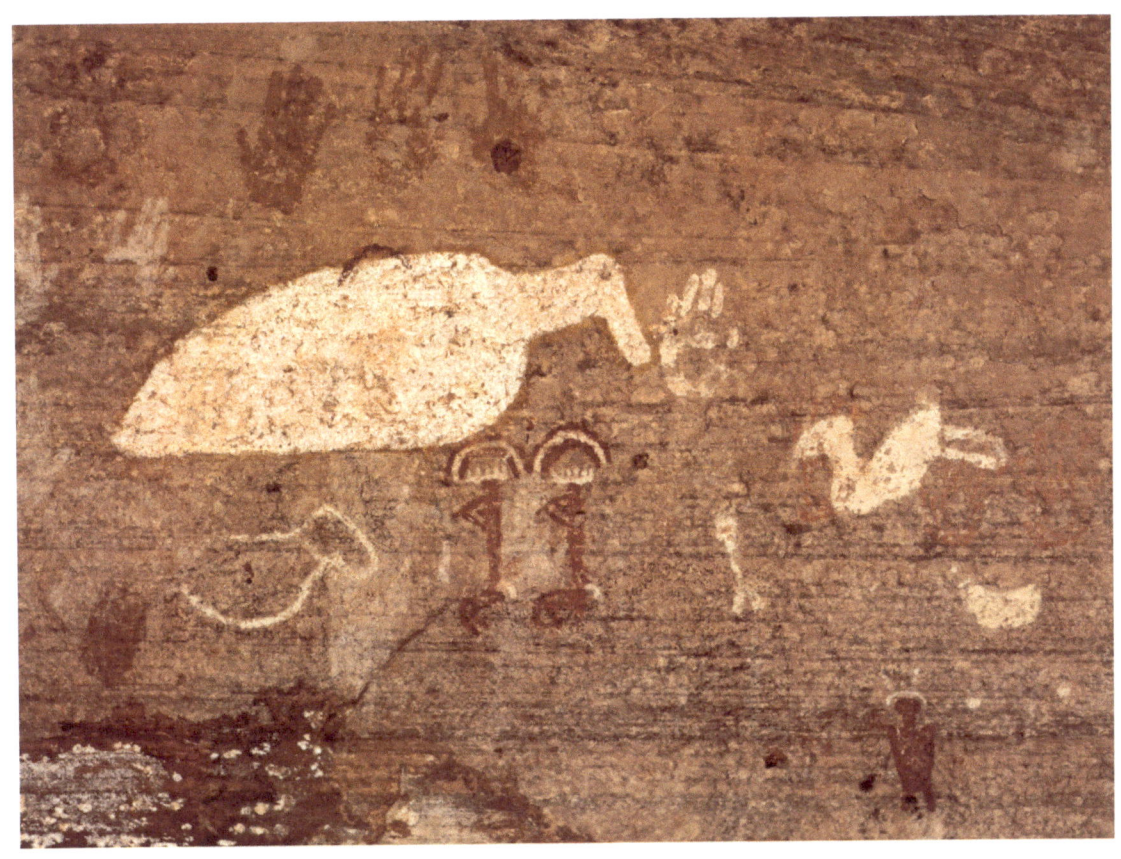

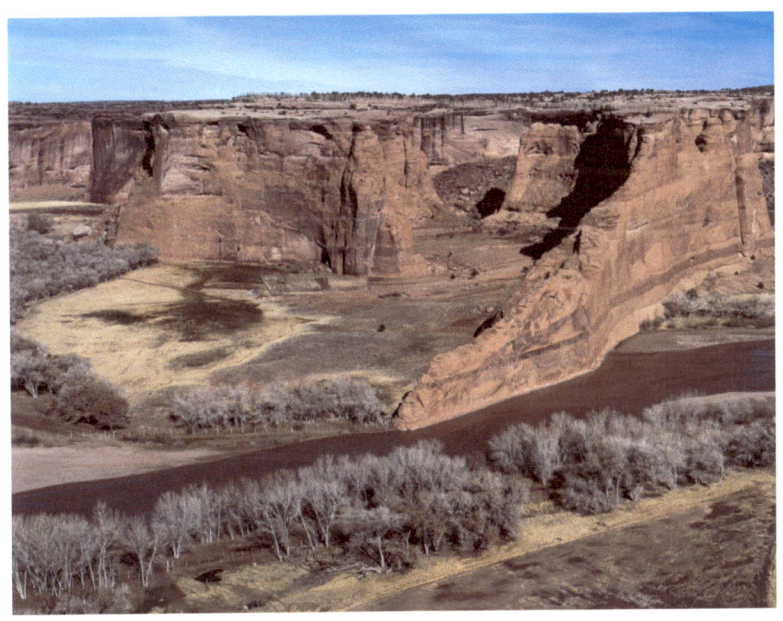

Bighorns Climbing

Pigment print
28 x 20 inches, 2013

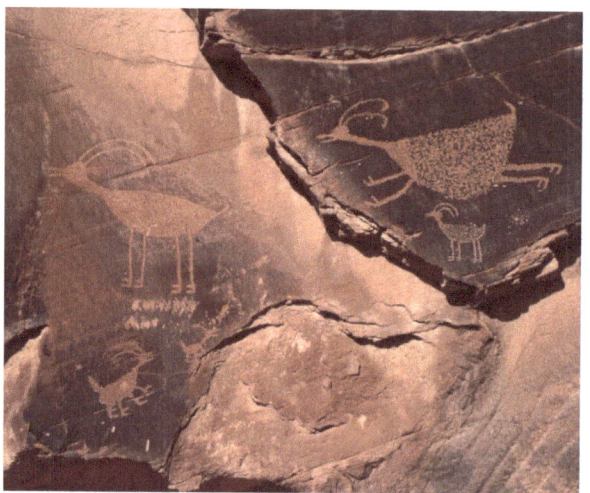

June 2013: *(upper right)* This is Monument Valley Navajo Tribal Park photographed from the deck of the Navajo-run View Hotel on a sunny summer afternoon. Even though Erma and I have been there countless times over four decades, we have never been disappointed by the awe-inspiring vistas.

(lower right) Fred Geary painted these Desert Bighorns at the Desert View Watchtower at the Grand Canyon in 1932.

March 1983: *(above)* Anasazi petroglyph examples of similar animals (A.D. 1050–1300) are etched in the rocks of the Mystery Valley section of Monument Valley.

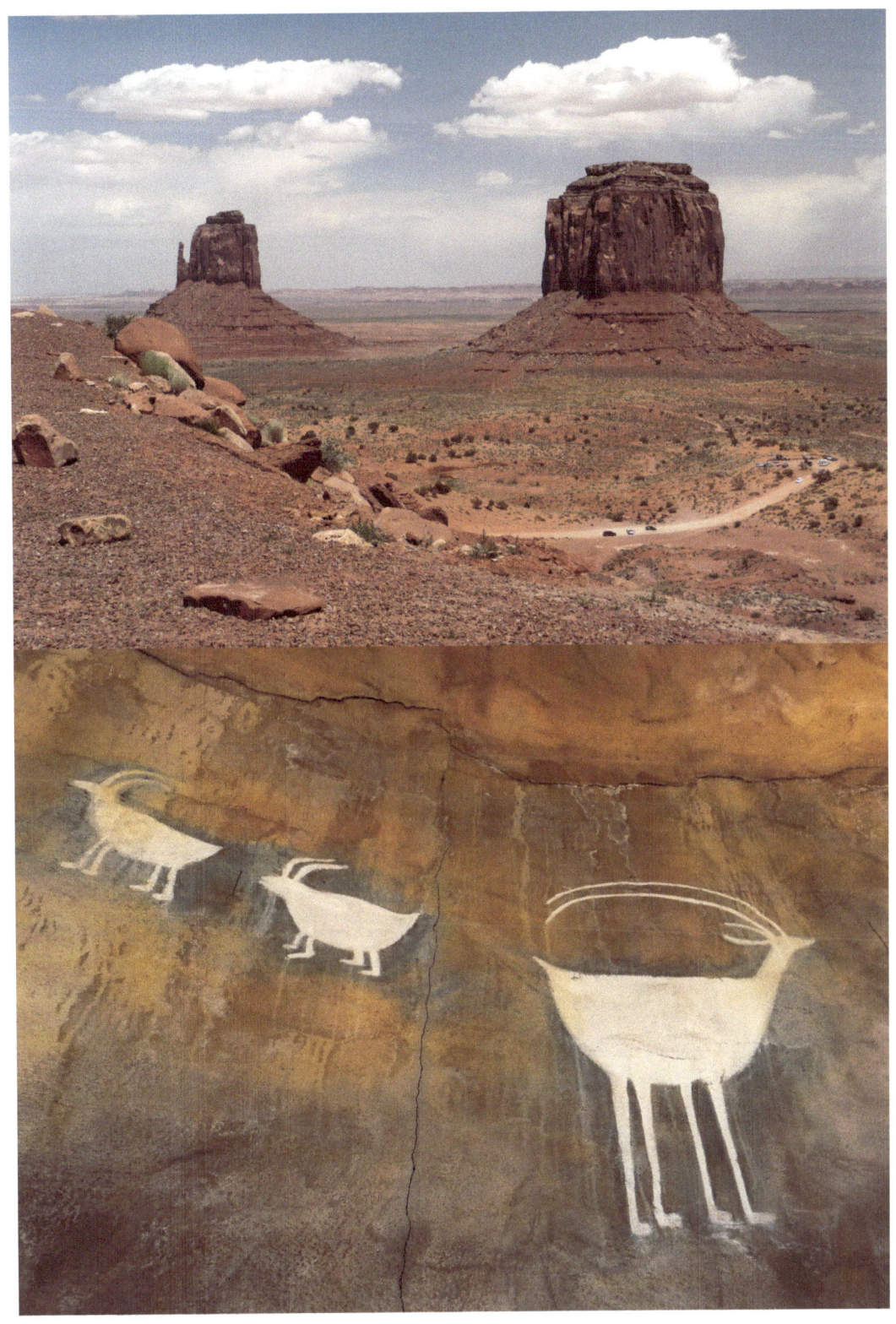

Reflected Monuments

Pigment print
26 x 22 inches, 2013

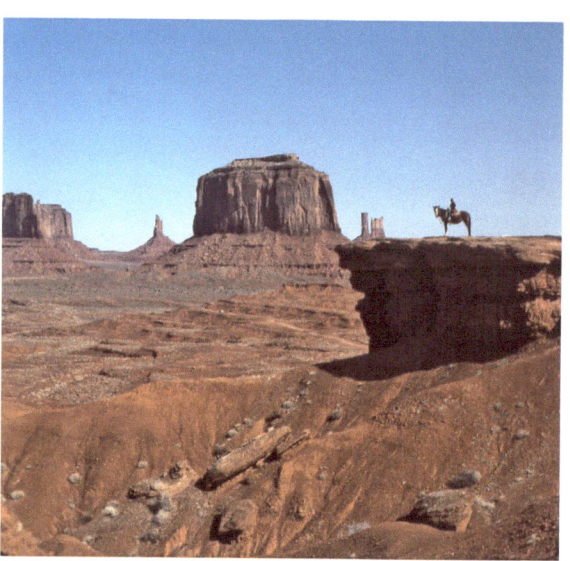

March 1983: (*above*) A Navajo boy and his pony view Monument Valley from a high perch near the Mystery Valley loop-road.

July 2004: (*right*) Chasing clouds through the monuments keeps me on my toes! Works upside down too.

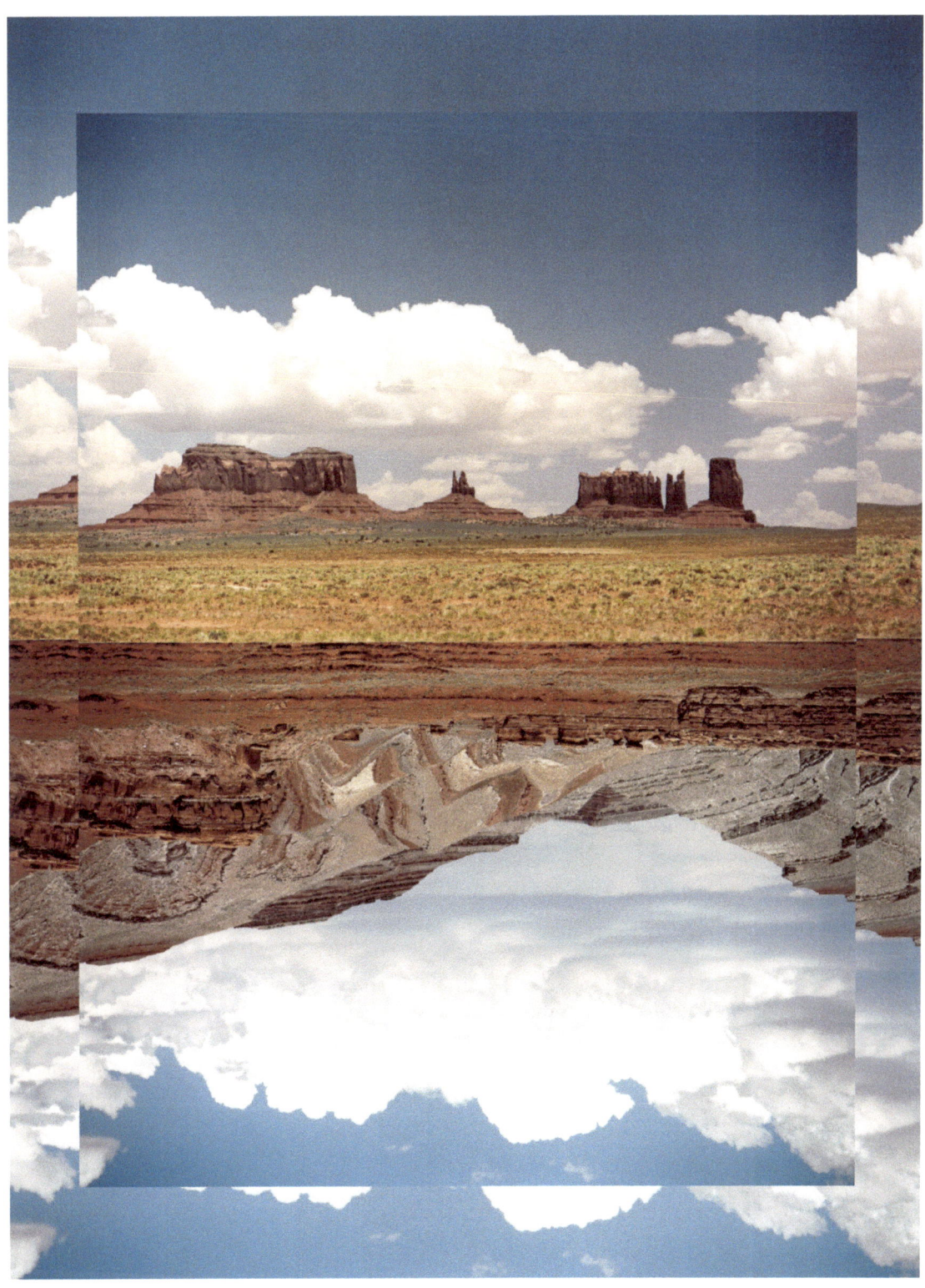

Sacred Summits

Pigment print
26 x 22 inches, 2013

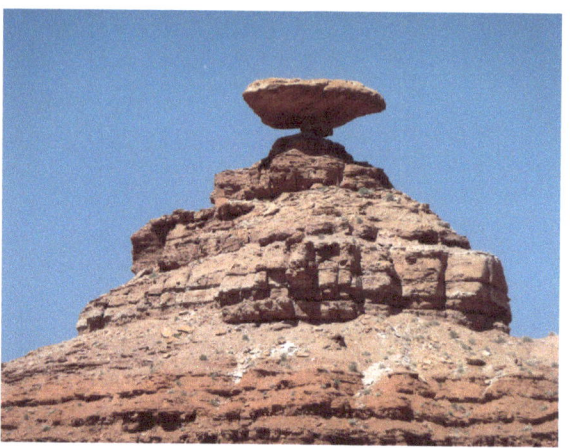

June 2013 and July 2004: *(above and lower right)* The balanced rock is 60-feet across—large enough to hold a house with an ample front yard. The striated terrain in the background rises from the banks of the meandering San Juan River on its approach to Mexican Hat.

(upper right) Fred Geary painted this pictograph of three birds perched on three peaks at the Desert View Watchtower in 1932.

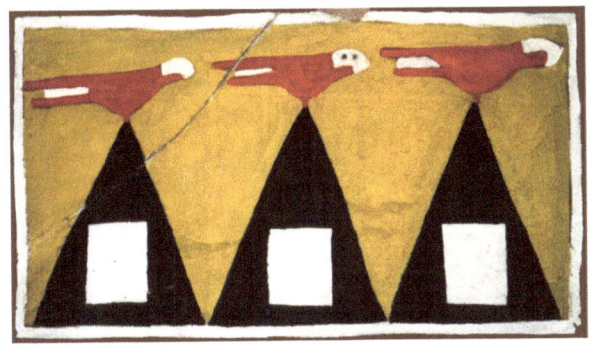

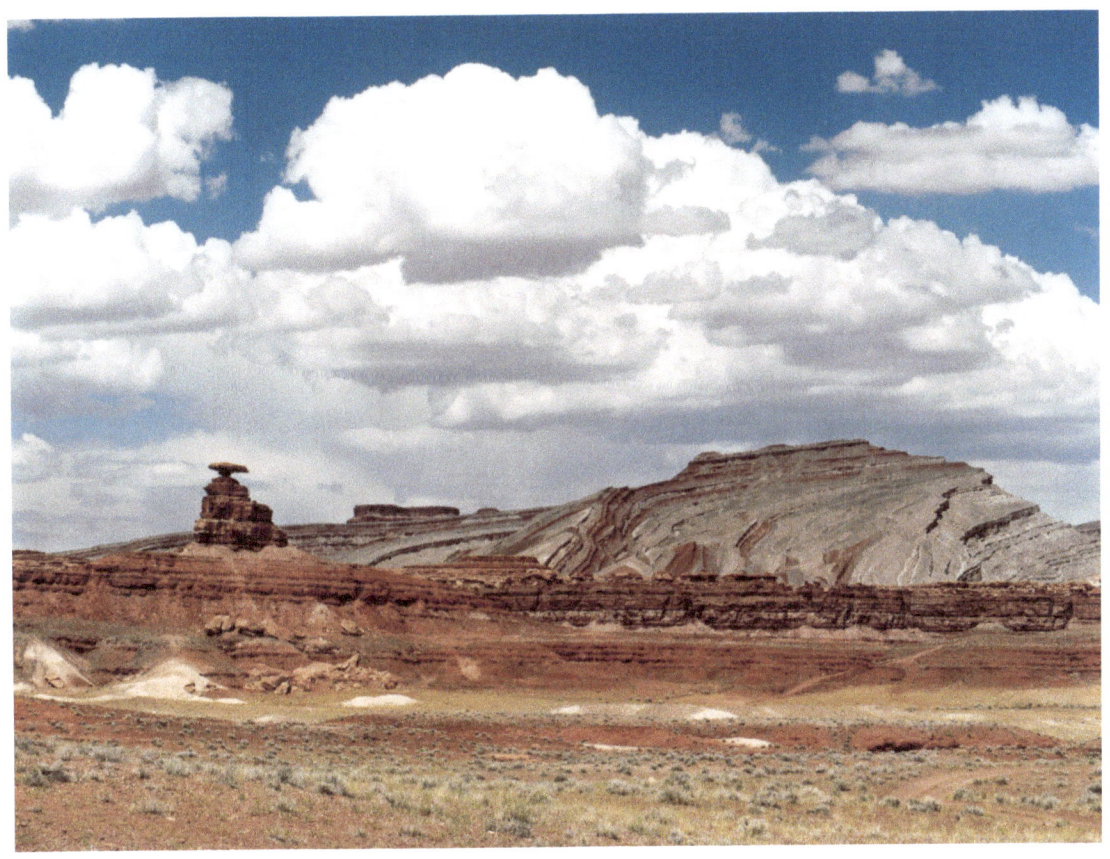

Thirteen Faces

Pigment print
26 x 22 inches, 2014

March 1982: Canyonlands National Park is an intimidatingly rugged preserve of flood-carved rocks and wind-borne sand in southeastern Utah. Steep trails threaten spills and quicksand awaits to suck-in any unwary traveler with a momentary lapse of concentration. Butch Cassidy hid here in the Robbers' Roost alcove—a difficult-to-get-to shelter in the Maze district—when he was running from the law.

(upper right) It was spring break when we rented a Jeep in Monticello and headed out in the early morning to find the *Thirteen Faces* pictographs we had heard about the prior year. We knew they were located in an unnamed canyon-spur in the Needles district and had sketchy directions from the young ranger at the trailer near the entrance. We were to watch for quicksand and try not to get lost, so we kept to the fast-moving water when crossing streams and tried to memorize distinctive landmarks along the way.

(lower right) Without too much trouble we found the *Thirteen Faces* by early afternoon in a small alcove hidden by a thicket. We were in dry sunny heat—a big change from chilly New York—so we spent the rest of the afternoon hiking and photographing near the pictographs.

These are life-size figures with mask-like faces—some 700 years old—in red hematite and white gypsum. Nine of the thirteen are clearly visible but only traces of the other four remain (shown are five of the best preserved). The alcove is low to the wash and flash floods have degraded the images over time. The paint application appears at least partially to be by finger streaks as evidenced on the red torsos of several figures. We quickly realized that we were standing on the exact spot where an ancient artist had labored centuries ago.

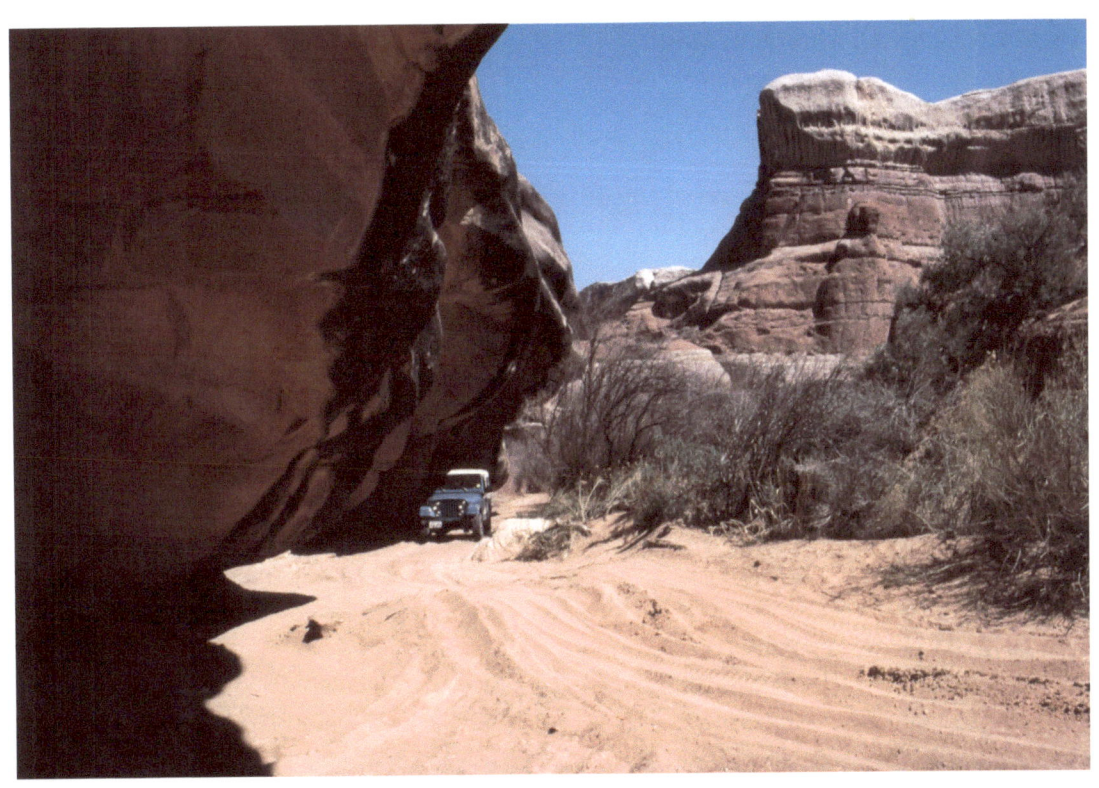

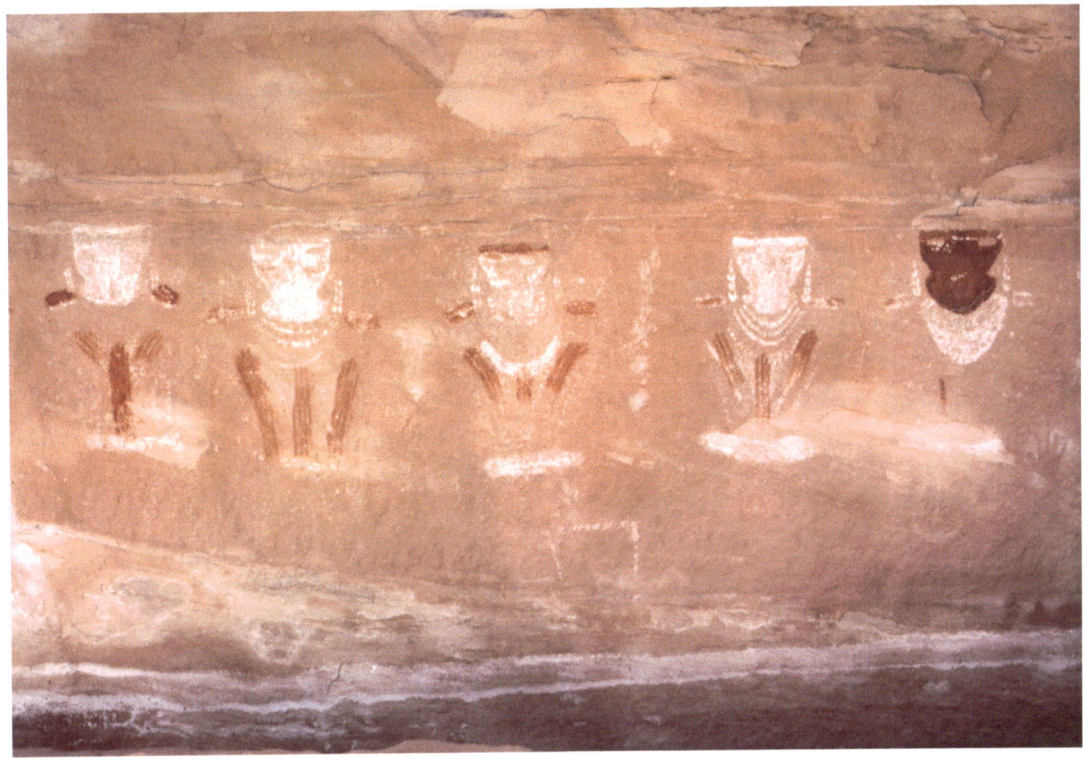

Angel Arch and All American Man

Pigment print
26 x 22 inches, 2013

March 1982: *(upper right)* In the late afternoon we drove from *Thirteen Faces* pictographs toward another canyon, hoping to find the famous Angel Arch. We decided to camp by a small stream because it would have been risky to four-wheel out after dark. We had sleeping bags in the Jeep but only some sticky-buns and trail snack to eat because we had just landed at Grand Junction and hadn't gotten around to doing our grocery shopping. Turns out the 70s-degree March daytime temperature quickly dropped to the 20s! The creek froze overnight and so did we. By the time the sun finally rose Erma was stiff as a wooden board. We hobbled to a sunny alcove to unfreeze but there was no way she was going to hike the mile to Angel Arch or anywhere else that morning. I took the cameras and found the trail to this spectacular vantage point for Molar Rock and Angel Arch. The inside of the arch rises 135 feet—high enough to span a 13-story building! Judge for yourself, but I think this is one of the most beautiful arches in the red-rock canyon country of eastern Utah. The sky was crystal clear that morning and vintage Kodachrome was in its element. By the time I got back to Erma's alcove several hours later her muscles had thawed and remarkably there were no aftereffects from the freezing night before.

March 1983: *(lower right)* More than 400 years before Betsy Ross designed the American Flag, a Native American painted the *All American Man* pictograph in Canyonlands National Park in patriotic red, white and blue. Erma and I went looking for it after a ranger directed us to take the Jeep-trail toward Angel Arch and then walk up the little creek for half a day. We were to watch for a big rock that looked like a loaf of bread rising from a wide field on our left. The rock was to have a long vertical crack with a hole at the bottom, and inside we would find the pictograph. Those of you who've been to Canyonlands know that this area is wilderness and the problem with these directions is that just about everything there is rock, rounded like loaves of bread.

We knew from our prior year's experience at Angel Arch to start early, so we left Monticello while it was still dark and got to the little creek soon after daybreak. It was cold and lightly snowing so we walked fast but not so quickly as to miss the "loaf of bread with the vertical crack." The surprise is that after six hours of ruling out rock after rock we actually found it! The circa 700-year-old life-size male figure, covered by a large shield, is surrounded by faint red handprints applied to the wall of a chamber about eight-feet above the ground. It was a pretty easy climb for me back then but Erma wisely chose to stay on solid ground. We lingered just long enough to shoot half a roll of Kodachrome and then quickly headed back, Erma with a 30-minute lead. By now the ground was snow-covered, just enough to make it white, and we knew we would be lucky to find the Jeep before dark. We eventually spotted it using our flashlights for the last mile or so. *(continued on page 52)*

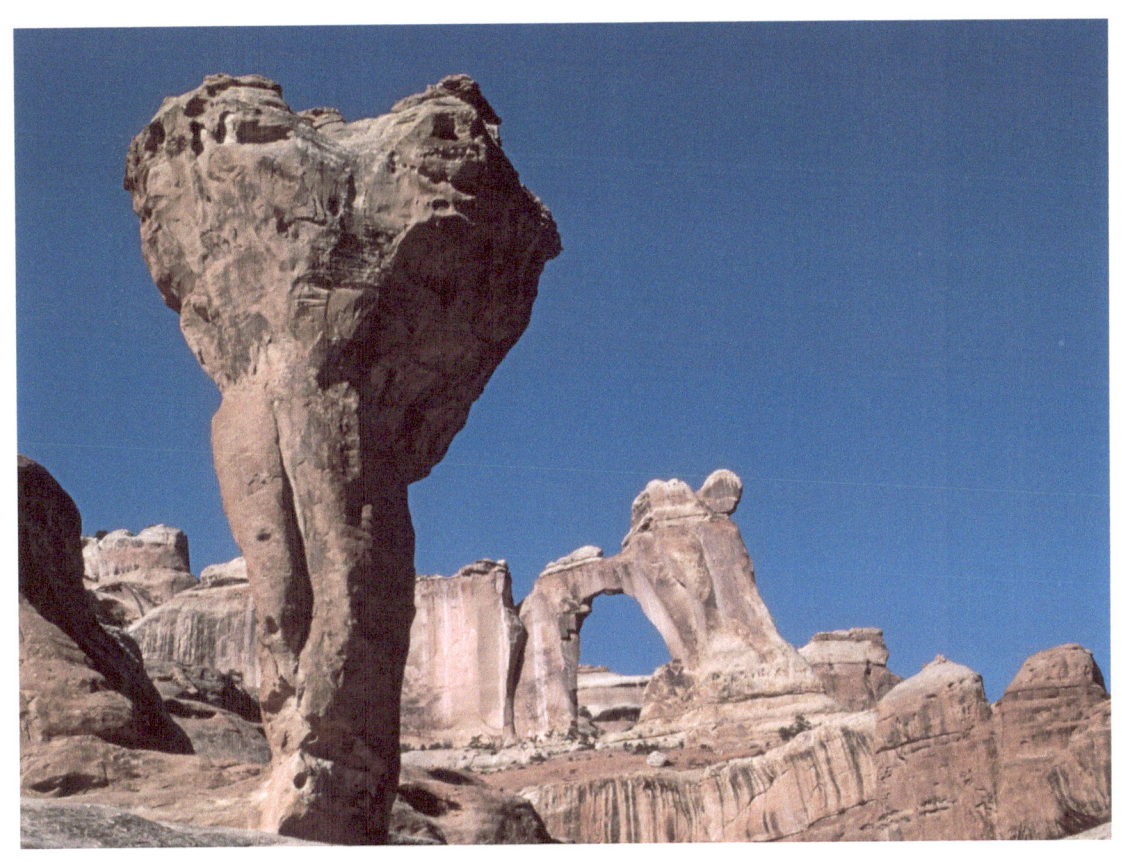

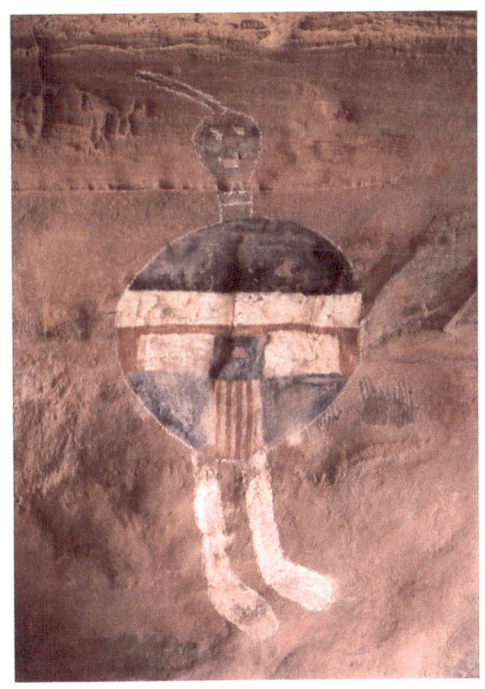

Fertile Furrows

Pigment print
26 x 22 inches, 2014

March 1983: *(continued from page 50)*
We had no desire to camp in the snow so we carefully retraced the 12-mile four-wheel trail to the highway with Erma holding the flashlight out her window to guide us through the slippery ruts. After nearly 40-years hiking the canyons the All American Man pictograph is still one of our favorites—maybe because we'll likely never see it again (now that the four-wheel trail is closed and you have to walk the entire 36-mile round trip). This is art for function's sake, a very un-modern concept. The shield is possibly for protection, and the decoration secondary. In shamanistic cultures, even an image of a shield can be imbued with protective power just like a physical shield.

◆ ◆ ◆

July 1988: *(lower right)* These three profiled figures are from the 45-mile long Nine Mile Canyon in northeastern Utah. Some 10,000 rock art sites line this canyon's walls—created by the Fremont and later the Ute inhabitants. Here are males with erect phalluses holding planting sticks and wearing backpacks, possibly filled with seeds. They look like Kokopelli flute players except that these figures grasp planting sticks instead of flutes. Planting sticks are fertility symbols as are the Kokopelli figures, who call rain with their flutes and plant seeds from their packs.

October 1985: *(upper right)* Modern day furrows sprout winter wheat while autumn clouds roll in over the Abajo Mountains.

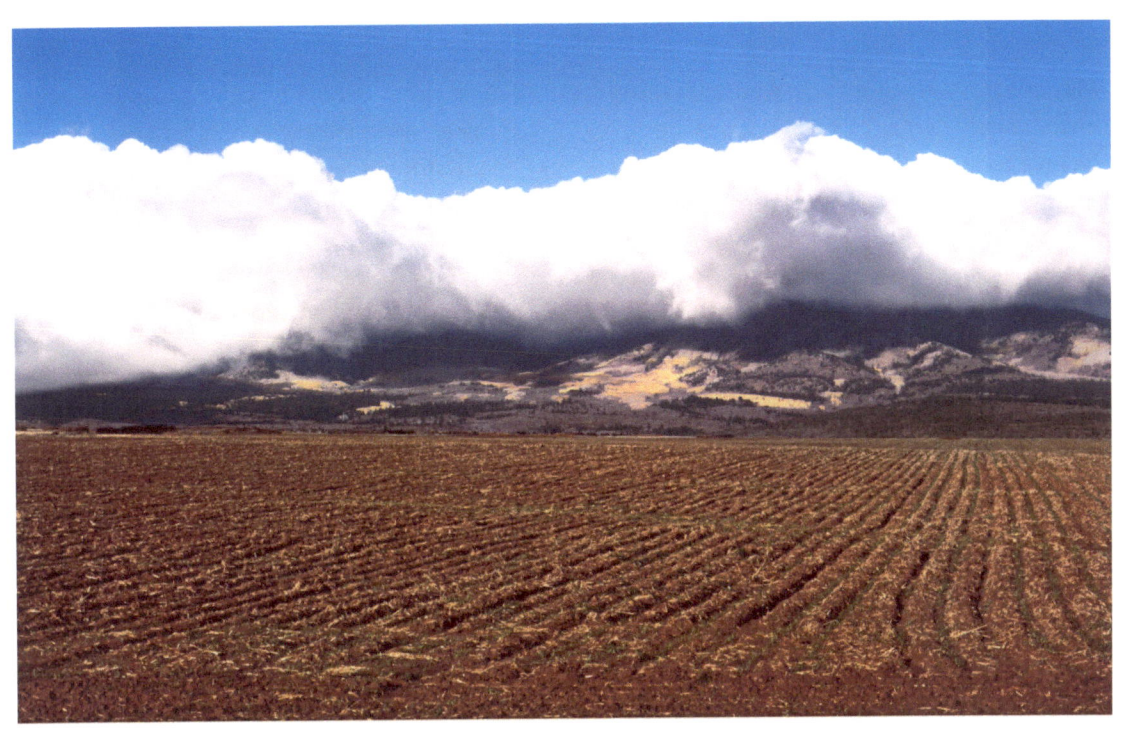

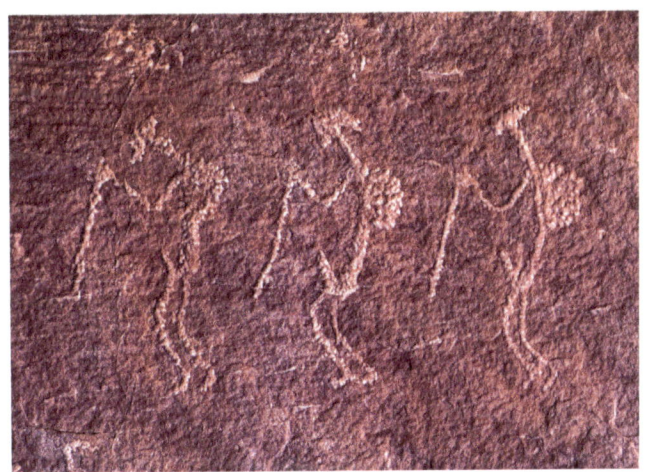

Silent Sentinel

Pigment print
26 x 22 inches, 2014

May 2002: Wyoming is a wild wilderness world encompassing America's first national park, Yellowstone (1872) and the high peaks of the Wind River Range of the Northern Rockies. The Eastern Shoshone and Northern Arapaho made this rugged region their home from as early as 11,000 years ago and many still live on the 3,532 square mile Wind River Reservation. Sacagawea of the Lewis and Clark expedition is buried here.

(lower right) The Mammoth Hot Springs terraced waterfall at the northern end of Yellowstone is one of the park's most photogenic features.

(upper right) This flying owl is part of a large petroglyph panel on Shoshone land of the Wind River Reservation.

(below) Short-membered anthropomorphic birds and animals levitate across a nearby cliff-face. The bullet holes are an unfortunate 20th century addition.

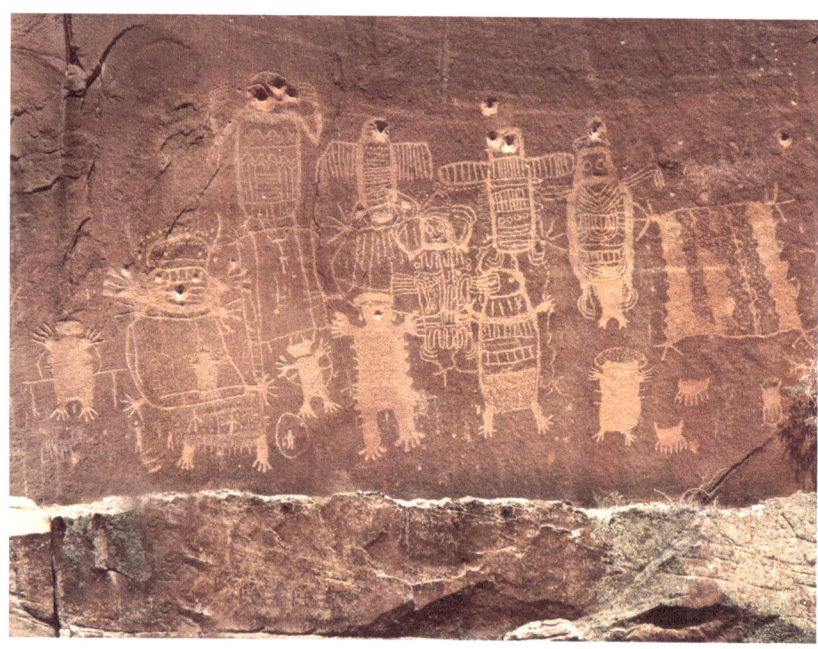

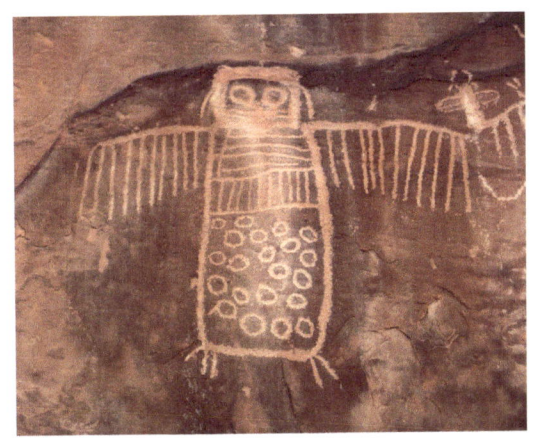

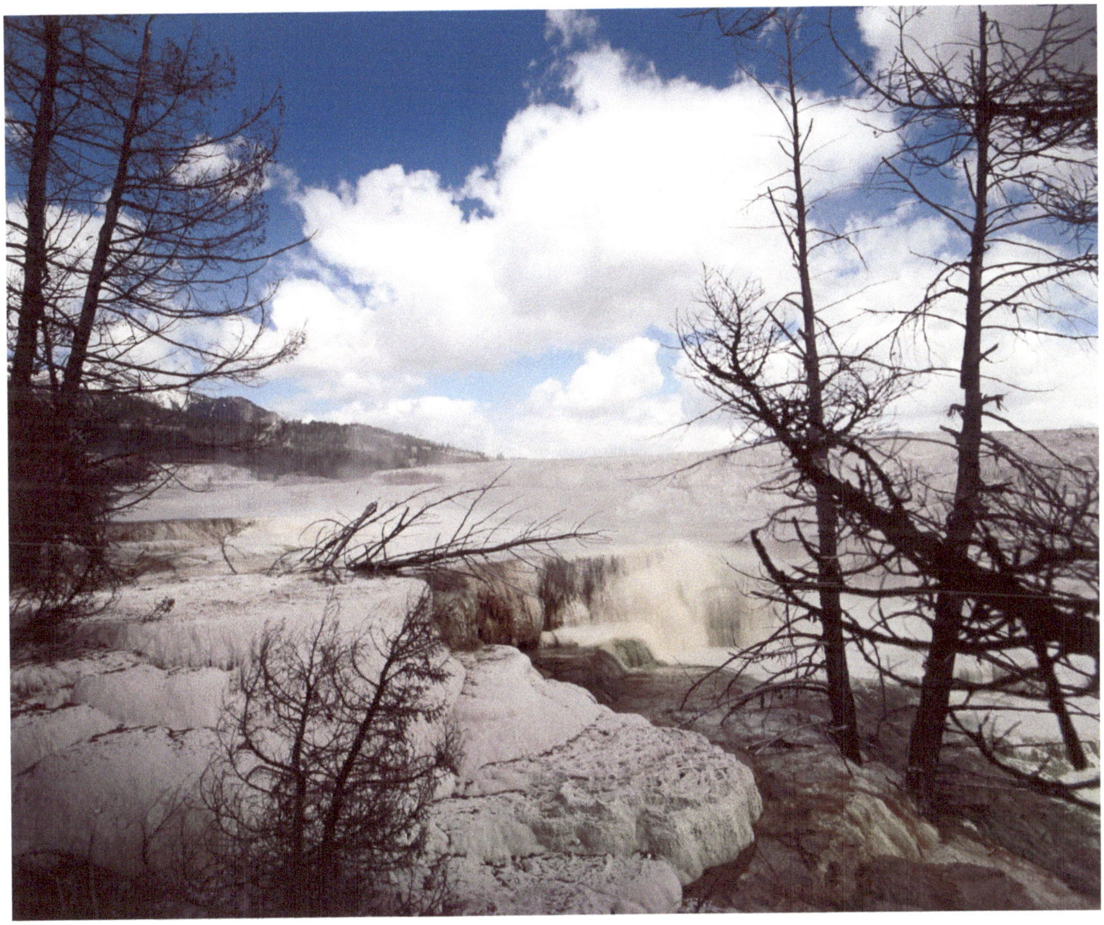

Born in the High Sierras

Pigment print
26 x 22 inches, 2014

May 2009: Sequoia National Park's ancient treasures are not limited to its groves of giant trees. Petroglyphs and pictographs are found there too, mostly hidden among the steep slopes and towering peaks.

(upper right) This petroglyph—outlined in chalk by an early explorer—is carved into the hard granite ceiling of a sheltered alcove next to a clear snow-fed stream. We don't know its intended purpose but to modern-day eyes it may have birthing meaning.

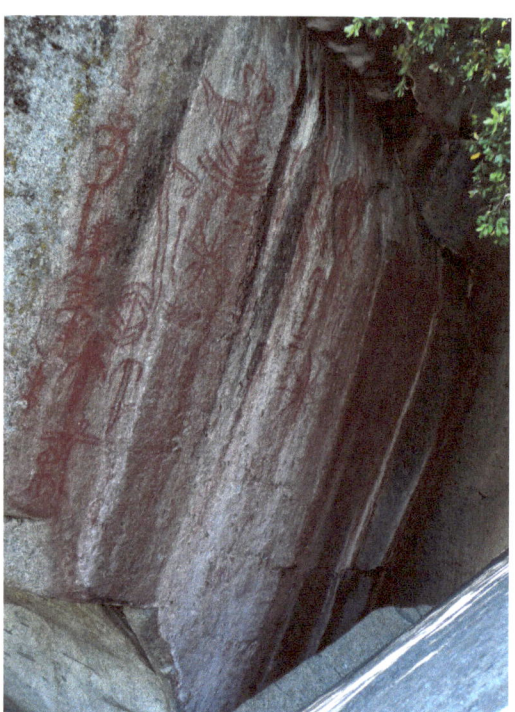

(above) These red painted pictographs on a nearby wall are intriguingly beautiful, even without knowing their intended meaning.

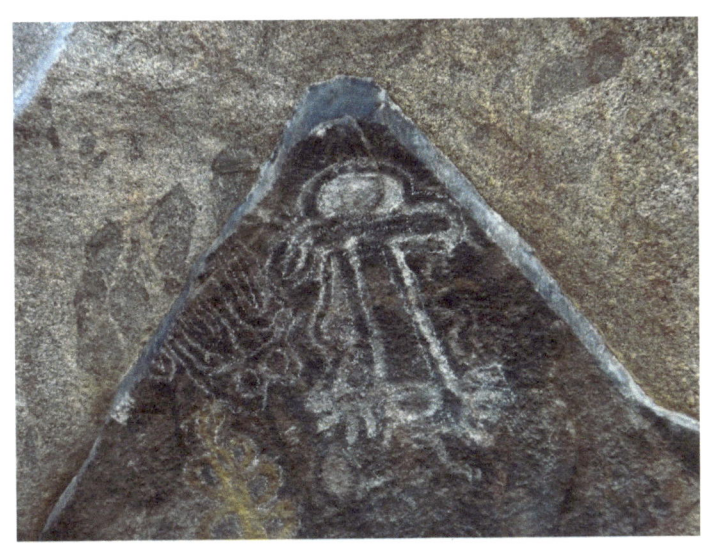

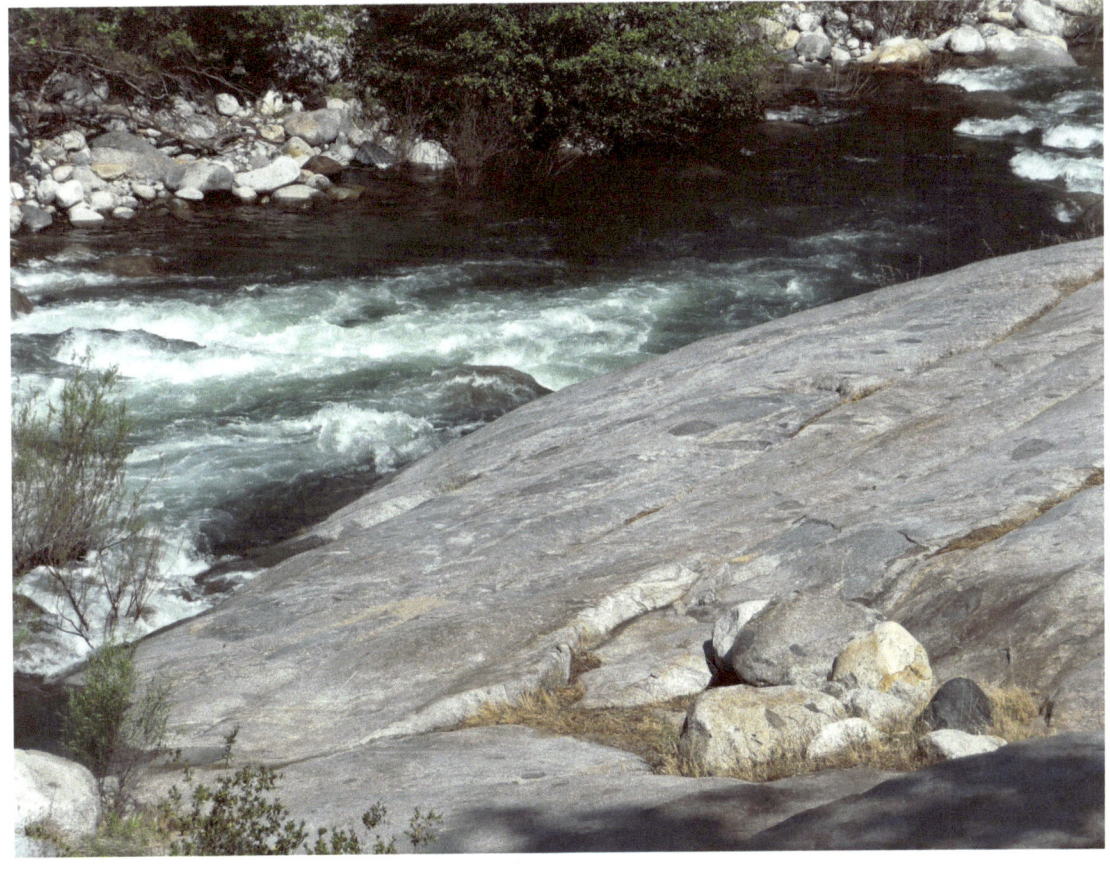

Rain at Winnemucca Lake

Pigment print
26 x 22 inches, 2013

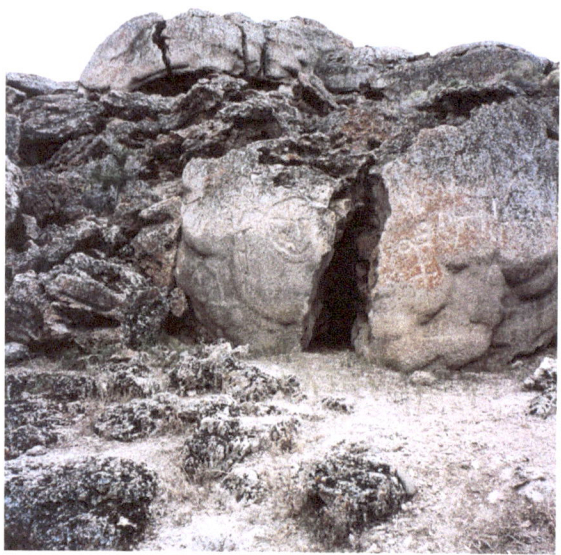

(above) Fractured tufa limestone creates evocatively rounded forms.

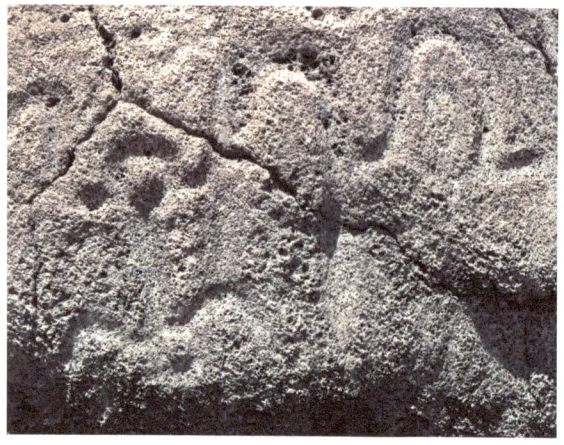

(above) A possible birthing depiction is in the lower left of this frame. The horseshoe-shaped symbol in the upper right corner may have similar symbolism.

The year 2013 made news in archeology circles with the approximate dating of America's oldest rock art site (10,500–14,800 years old, Dr. Larry Benson, et al). Once underwater, and now exposed, geologists used deposits left by the changing water levels over time to estimate the era that the engravings would have been made.

June 1993: *(upper right)* Now Winnemucca Lake is a mostly dry salt flat in the desert east of the Sierra Nevada Mountains.

(lower right) A mangled mass of tufa limestone rises from a small hill on what was once lake bottom. Ancients carved symbols into the tufa's soft porous surfaces and arranged a ring of rocks in a flat-bottomed depression in the center of the fractured boulders. The designs on the rocks are mostly abstract; large zigzags, chains of circles and rake-like plant forms interspersed with an occasional sunburst or shield.

The site is on the Pyramid Lake Indian Reservation, governed by the Paiute tribe. Access is restricted because of vandalism concerns.

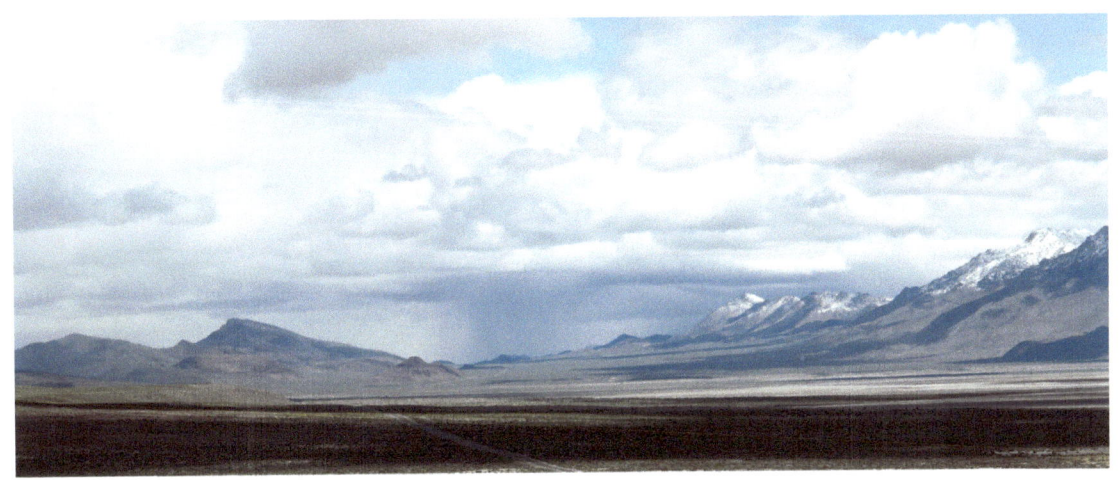

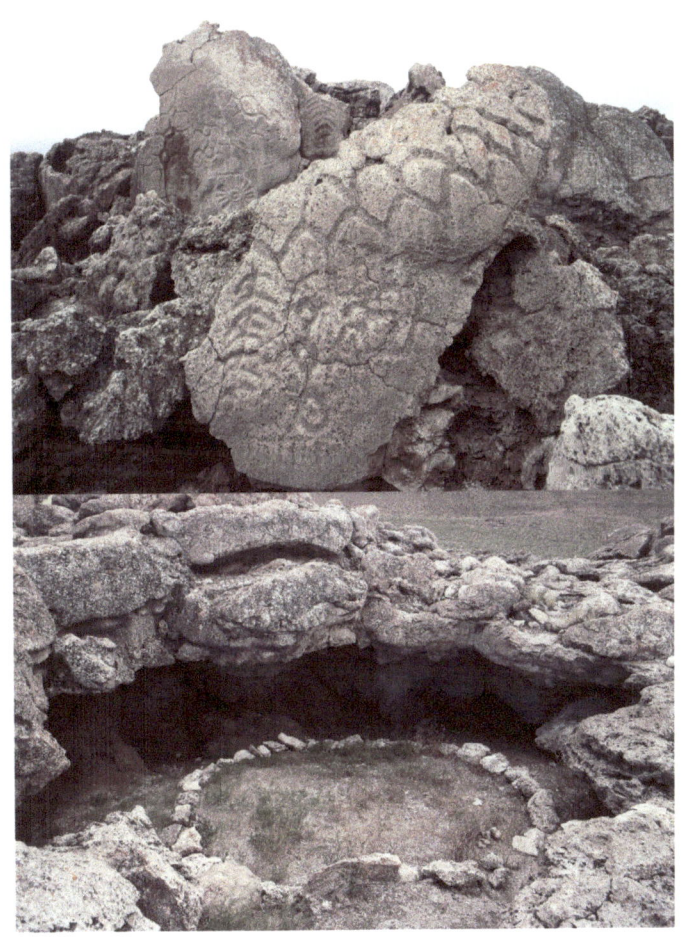

Desert Blossoms

Pigment print
26 x 22 inches, 2013

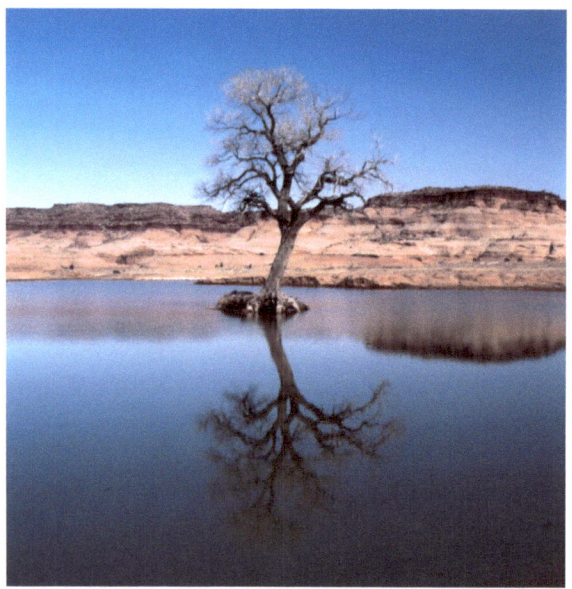

March 1983: *(above)* This old cottonwood stands in the middle of a dammed-up wash in the tiny Navajo village of Oljato, not far from Monument Valley. During the March snowmelt it fills with water but by mid-summer it's dry.

June 2013: *(right)* Just a plane ticket to Albuquerque, a few hundred miles in a rental car and a sturdy pair of hiking boots—all worth it for a colorful picture.

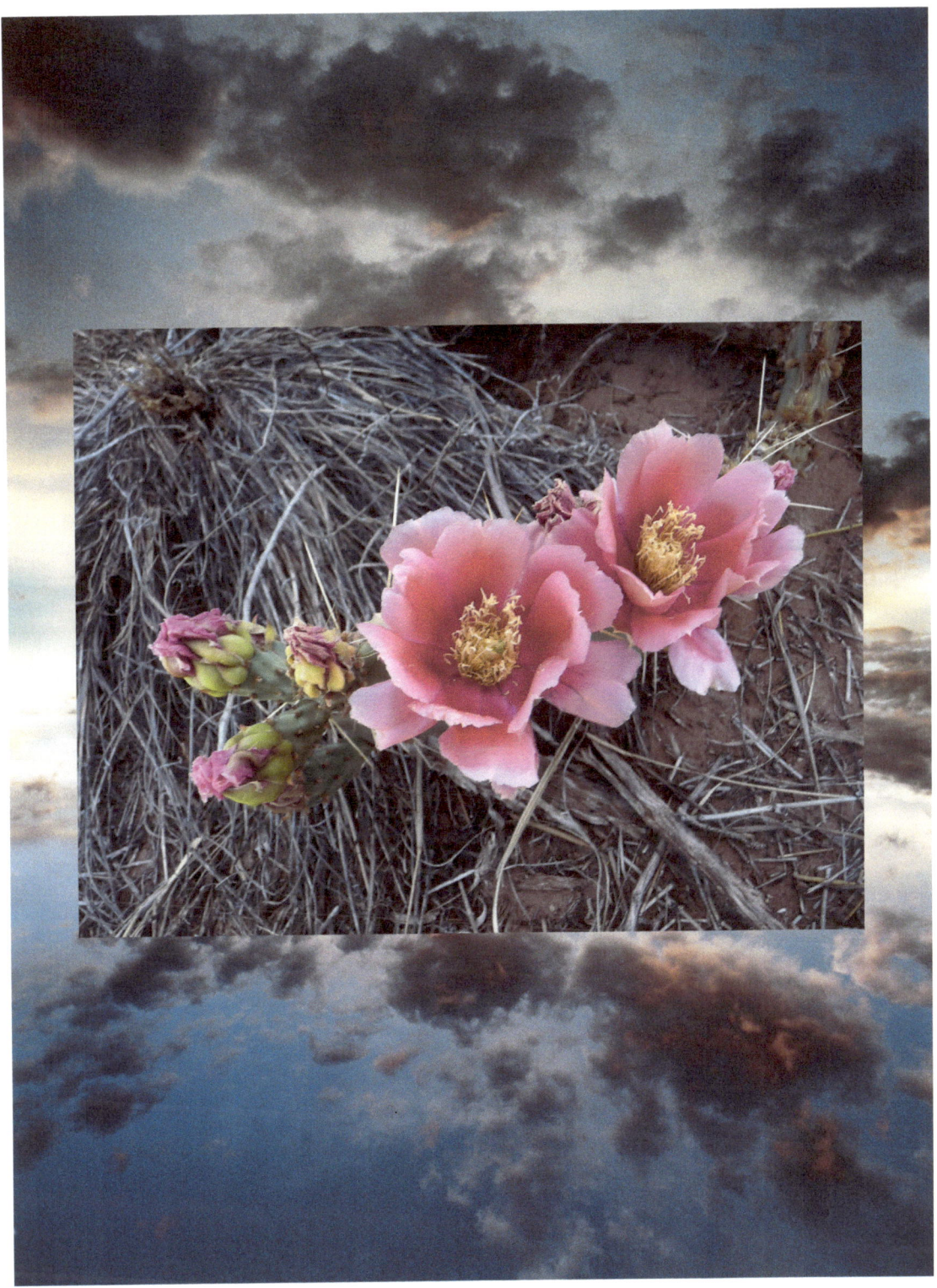

Anasazi Sky

Pigment print
26 x 22 inches, 2013

August 1978: *(lower right)* First rays of morning sun transform the northern Navajo Nation's Navajo Mountain into America's version of Ayres Rock, outlining its flattened form above the waking desert land. Wind-borne sand creates a crimson spectrum on this untamed topography of canyons and mesas some 66 to 138 million years in the making. The mountain is sacred to the Hopi who call it "Heart of the Earth," and to the Navajo who call it "Naatsis'áán—Head of the Earth." Bulging upward to 10,388 feet, it is a hefty mass of laccolithic rock, visible on a clear day from 90 miles away.

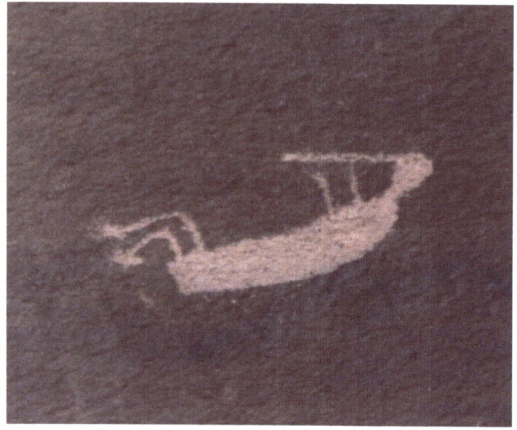

October 1987: *(upper right)* Ancient art marks countless canyons throughout this alluring domain, incised by Anasazi inhabitants some 1,500 years ago. The petroglyphs comprise a story written by long-departed authors who left no Rosetta stone for their decipherment. Nonetheless, the serpents, bighorns, Kokopellis, duck, and spiral connected by a crooked line to a human with upraised arms were all native to this place. They still create a compelling composition even without the message they were intended to communicate. They are placed high on the wall of a small canyon, requiring a long trek across a sandy mesa to get there. On one visit I tried to drive the four-wheel trail to the rim and got stuck in the sand on the way out—a lesson that sometimes it's just better to walk.

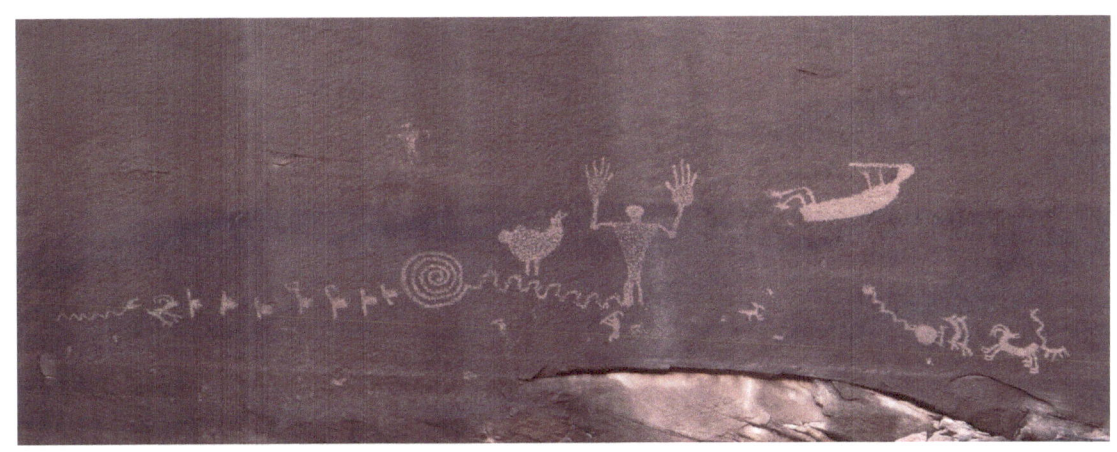

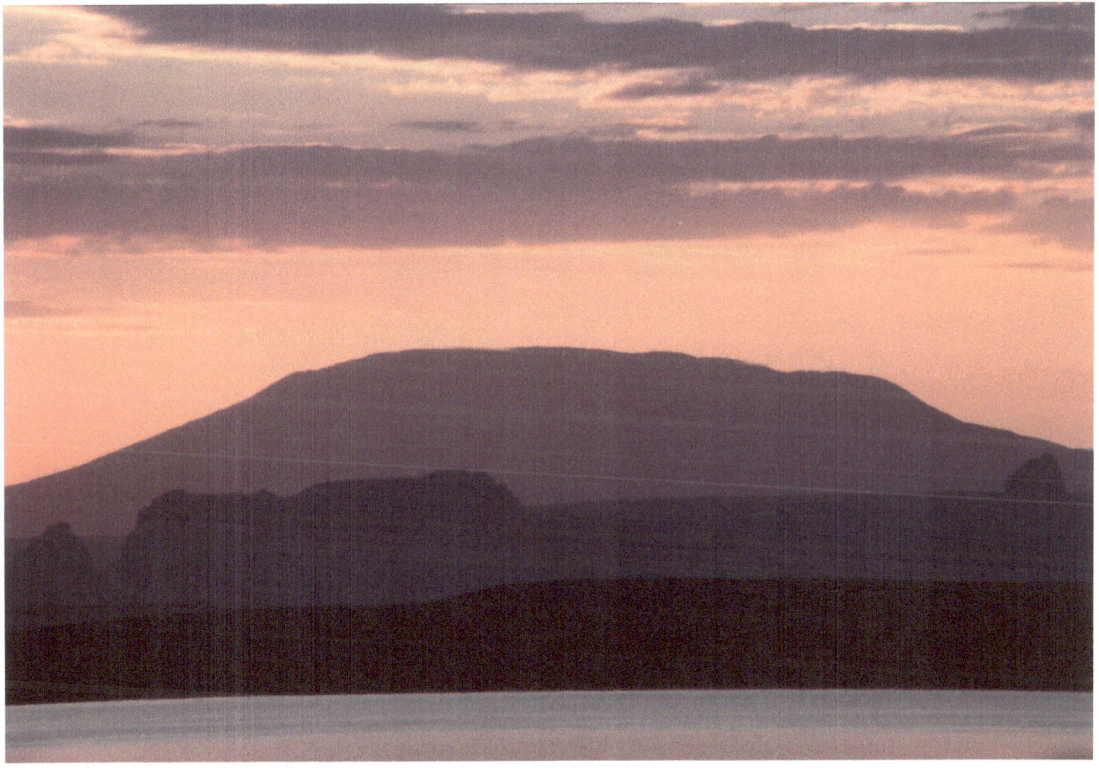

63

Mittens in the Morning

Pigment print
26 x 22 inches, 2013

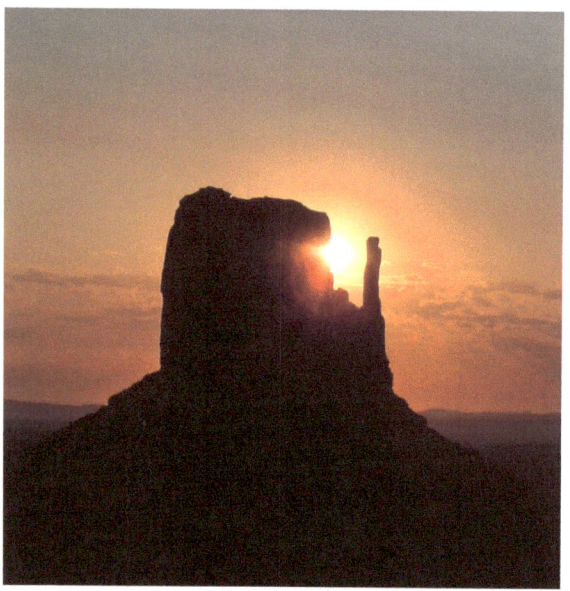

June 2013: Early risers catch crimson colors and a warm dry breeze over Monument Valley's famous pair of Mittens. Our first time there was 1977 and the view is never short of breathtaking!

(upper right) Fred Geary painted this dragonfly pictograph at the Desert View Watchtower in 1932.

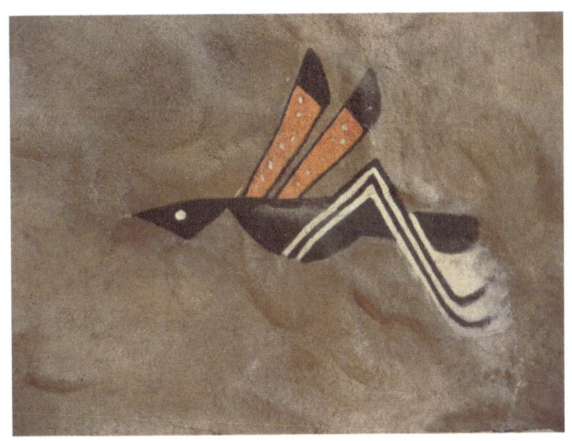

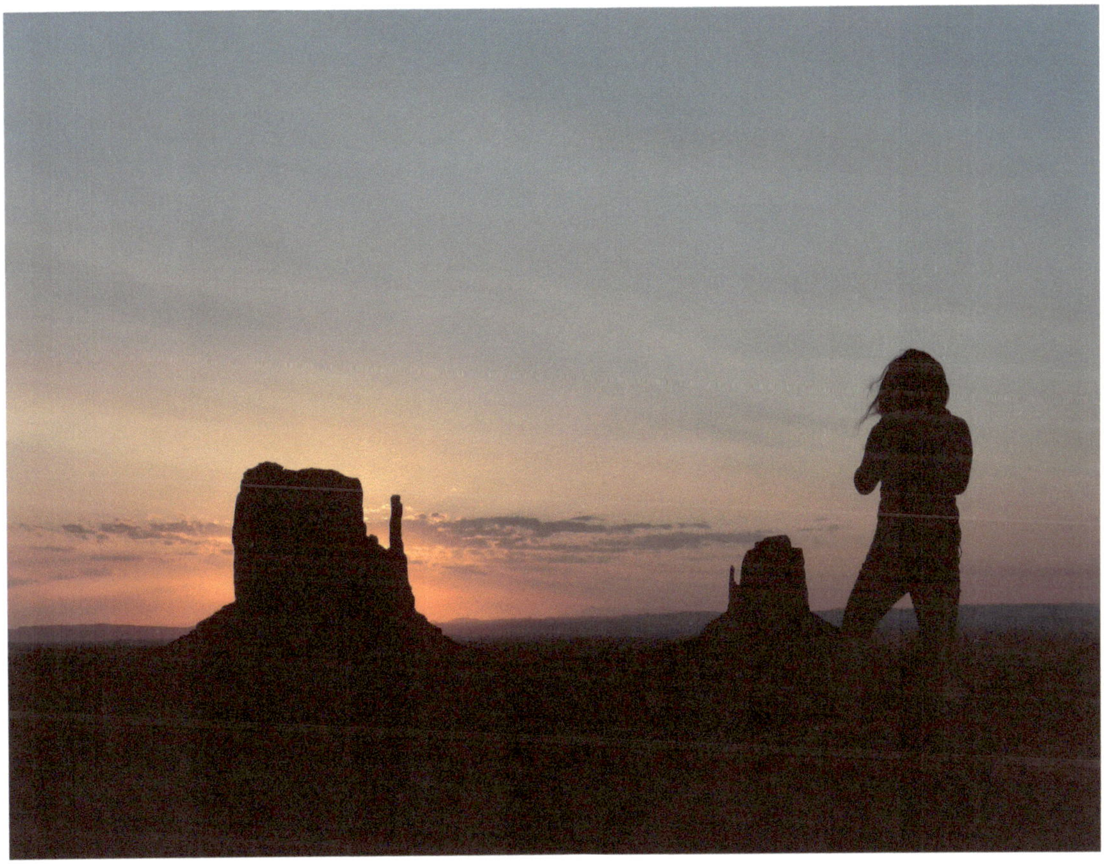

Stormy Sky

Pigment print
26 x 22 inches, 2013

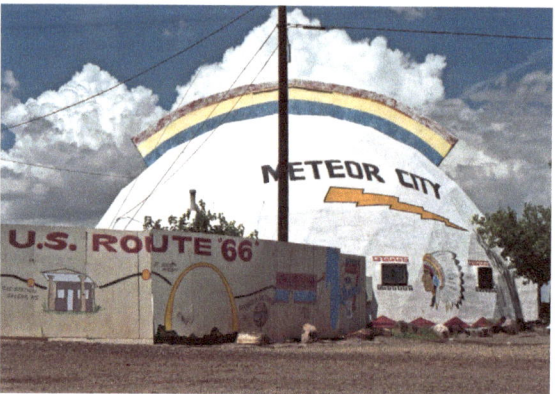

July 2004: *(lower right)* These concrete teepees contain real motel lodgings but after a peek inside Erma and I opted to stay in a regular rectangular room. Holbrook, Arizona is one of our favorite towns on the Route 66 Mother Road for mid-century nostalgic kitsch—and for style, the '59 Chevy is still hard to beat.

(upper right) Fred Kabotie painted these pictographs in the Desert View Watchtower at the Grand Canyon in 1932. Stepped rainclouds, a rainbow and serpents from the Hopi Rain Dance encircle a symbol of the four cardinal directions.

(above) The journey down iconic Route 66 takes you past dinosaur bones, petrified landscapes and fragments of rock blasted from the three-quarter-mile wide meteor crater. Even the futuristic inventor and visionary Buckminster Fuller left his mark via the geodesic-domed Meteor City gift shop.

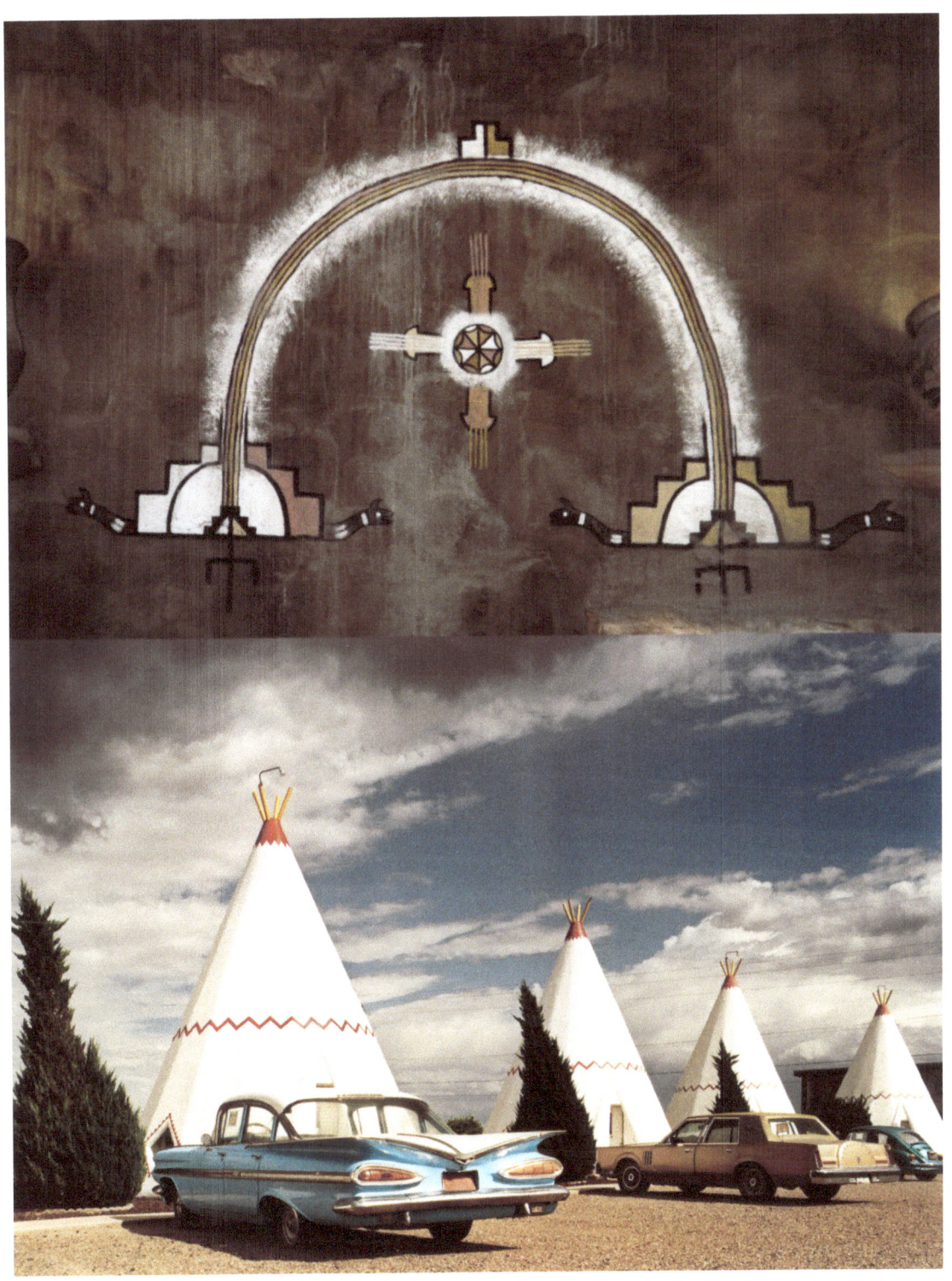

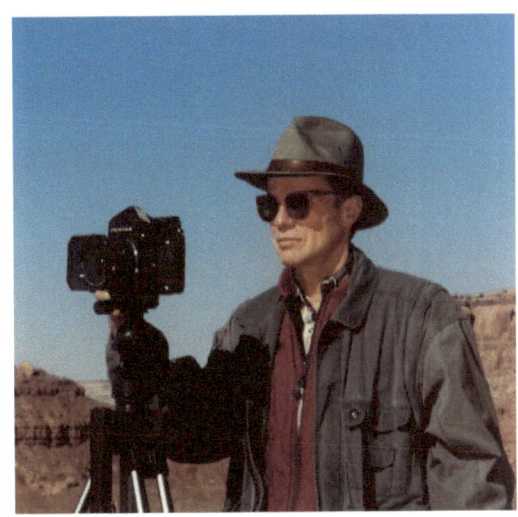

photo by Erma Martin Yost, 1997

About the Photographer

Leon Yost is a professional documentary photographer who has worked as a location scout for the BBC and is published in *Time-Life Books, American Photo, The New York Times* and many other publications. He began documenting Native American rock art when he and his painter-wife, Erma Martin Yost, made their first tour through the Southwest in 1976. Now, after four decades of carrying cameras through countless canyons they still make annual pilgrimages looking for new discoveries. Yost has had 25 solo gallery exhibitions, and two solo museum exhibitions: at the Jersey City Museum in 1979 and the San Diego Museum of Man in 1997. You may contact him at ermaleon@gmail.com or follow him on facebook.com/leon.yost

Ed McCormack, of ARTspeak magazine writes, "*Yost brings an exquisitely refined pictorial sensibility to bear on the sacred sites he photographs, to imbue them with a haunting spiritual resonance.*"